Believing

D0937308

Believing

Eugene Kennedy

ORBIS BOOKS
Maryknoll, New York 10545

Founded in 1970, Orbis Books endeavors to publish works that enlighten the mind, nourish the spirit, and challenge the conscience. The publishing arm of the Maryknoll Fathers and Brothers, Orbis seeks to explore the global dimensions of the Christian faith and mission, to invite dialogue with diverse cultures and religious traditions, and to serve the cause of reconciliation and peace. The books published reflect the views of their authors and do not represent the official position of the Maryknoll Society. To learn more about Maryknoll and Orbis Books, please visit our website at www.maryknollsociety.org.

Library of Congress Cataloging-in-Publication Data

Kennedy, Eugene C.
    Believing / Eugene Kennedy.
      pages cm
    ISBN 978-1-62698-017-4
    1. Faith.   I. Title.
    BV4637.K43 2013
    234'.23--dc23

                                                                2012048586

I have always dedicated my books
to my wonderful wife, Sally,
and she joins me now in dedicating this book
to
Vickie and Mike Leach,
True Lovers / True Believers

Contents

Introduction

This is a book of commonplace thoughts, the kind we all have from time to time, about what, whom, and, at times, whether we believe at all. Believing is a traditional concern for anybody interested in religion or in life; indeed, believing is a profoundly human characteristic, a note by which men and women are defined and distinguished from other species. We do not have a choice about believing any more than we do about breathing, and each is equally important for our survival. What and how we believe prompt other questions that, as we know from history and psychology, we continue to answer in a wide variety of ways.

Believing is a problem for the theologian on a theoretical level, but it is a practical one for all of us on an everyday level. During the course of some research on American priests, which I was involved in many years ago, I became aware of how hard it is for most people to speak clearly about what they believe in. It is far simpler to describe what we believe about. We may recite the articles of the creed, but do they sum up or express the mystery of belief? Are these, for many of us, the texts we must affirm to be members of a religious group, the codes, as it were, through

which we gain entrance to the religious group? Does our assent
to them fulfill requirements, or do they allow us to discover or express deep personal longings or understandings of our transcendent
experiences?

These latter challenges—everyday ones rather than mystical
flights—are largely a function of the symbolism and language of
believing. It may be that we are so estranged from a religious language that speaks effectively to and of our experience that we
resemble strangers in a foreign land—limited in our capacity to
express our faith not because of a failure to believe, but because
we lack the language in which to do it effectively. To explore the
nature and function of believing in the personality and to find the
words and signs that enable men and women to sense and sing
of the richness of their need and power to believe is perhaps the
dominant religious challenge of the age. I hope that this book helps
to define that challenge rather than to answer it; it provides a sense
of direction for all of us who are concerned with the meaning
of life and with lighting the path teeming with men and women
questing, like Arthurian knights, for the Grail of belief.

This book is essentially two parts. In the first half, I reflect on
the nature of believing in the lives of men and women. Although
I reviewed the literature of psychological research in preparation
for this task, I have placed the fruits of this search into the context
of the convictions about the need to believe, which have grown
in me as I have been privileged to work closely with many different human persons. To argue for the central significance of believing may seem as conventional as defending baseball, the flag, and
mother love. If you think about it for a moment, however, there
has been a great deal of argument about the purity and virtue of
even these formerly unquestioned aspects of our heritage. So it is
always worthwhile to look again at familiar matters, or at responses

that seem second nature to us, to see if we can develop a deeper and perhaps more nuanced understanding of them.

This is especially true in the era of fashionable atheism in which the modern equivalent of the nineteenth-century evangelist of unbelief, Robert Ingersoll, would lay his gleaming watch on the speaker's rostrum and dare God to strike him dead by the time the second hand swept sixty seconds off the face of his timepiece.

Today, journalists, such as the late Christopher Hitchens, have gone to their deaths holding on to their protests against God's existence. God would understand a troubled and suffering person who, like Hitchens, had protested life and the fullness with which believers, such as Mother Teresa, lived it in his books and articles. There was something poignant in the searching that lay beneath his smashing of every idol he encountered, as if he knew that if he smashed enough of them he would find something behind one of them that spoke to the yearning he layered over with cynicism.

Modern times are filled with the snap-fingered dismissal of God that goes with atheism. Yet the God they dismiss—a brooding and demonic figure giving people life and piling it carelessly with loss and pain—is not the God of the great religions. Still, as we shall see, it is normal for people to test their belief systems rather than to accept them as on a par with the grandfather's clock and the bracelets or cufflinks that they inherit from their parents. Examining our faith, asking questions rather than thinking we have all the answers, is a necessary stage in the maturation of our faith.

It is the same way with believing, drained of any hint of full-bodied vigor through the long and almost unconscious historical process by which beliefs are reduced to the dry intellectualized mantras of dogma. Faith, however, is a function of the whole rather than a part of the person; men and women are eager to believe, but they want something substantial to give themselves to, something that matches their joys and sorrows, something that sounds a call to believe deeply rather than just to close their eyes and cling in the deep waters of life to the side of the battered lifeboat of old-time religion.

Everybody, including the atheist, believes in some framework or explanatory system, some philosophy or scheme of purpose. People are often reluctant to examine their belief systems too closely for fear that they will find too many inconsistencies or that they may find that they no longer really believe the things they were taught, and then what would they do? Does belief become talismanic, on the edge of superstition, but something we are so accustomed to that we hold on even if its rewards are less robust than they once were? In the second half, I examine this bridge to see if it will bear our weight and where it may really lead. We cannot cross that bridge off our itinerary as it leads to religious maturity. There is no other way to get there. The challenge at this stage may be to let older formulations drop away and to seek a new and higher level integration of our beliefs with our life experiences.

Such an examination is necessary because, as in anything else of importance in life, we cannot believe just because someone else tells us to, and we cannot let somebody else, even if he is the pope, believe for us. As we must love from our own hearts and speak words that are our own, we must believe for ourselves. The outcome of such a search need not be frightening; in fact, it is essential if our faith is to remain fresh and to grow. To keep matching our experiences and our beliefs with each other, in order to draw them more closely together so that we may achieve the wholeness that living faith does provide, is an essential and indispensable religious action.

In order to carry this out, we need the assistance of organized religion; we need a church sensitive to the human struggle to believe that speaks not only the truths of faith to us, but that joins with us as we seek to express our faith. One of the purposes of this book is to reinforce the importance of the institutional church and to discuss its opportunities positively rather than to criticize it for its failings. The perennial challenge to organized religion is to sift through the ordinary events of our lives and to make them transparent to transcendence for us.

That is not accomplished by handing someone a catechism to read: here, you will find everything you need in here; memorize it and be saved. The work of the institutional church is to seek out the formulations of faith that match rather than contradict the experiences of ordinary people. Faith does not need to explain or provide an understanding of everything that befalls us in our lives.

Although some people demand it, the task of organized religion is not to give meaning to life. It is meant rather to help us deepen our sense of being alive, of making sure that we do not miss life even in its painful and bewildering moments. Faith does not solve, but rather it opens us to the mystery of being alive.

The questions that trouble many adults are these: Will the church be there for our children and grandchildren as it has been for us? Will it seek to live in and with them in the unfolding future, or will it seek refuge in the vacuum sealed past? Will the church be alive and present as younger generations, beset with ever new challenges, find a church that speaks the language of faith and provides the symbols of belief that can sustain them?

I think that the belief needs of men and women run painfully deep and that the church must not retreat into a comforting past, but rather proceed into the future seeking a better understanding of what it believes so that it can provide the sacramental environment and the human community in which faith can come vigorously to life for believers.

Years ago, the psychologist Carl Rogers told me that he had come to believe that he was wiser than his intellect, that he knew more than he seemed to know. He referred to levels of understanding and response that are deep within his total personality as they are within us, the "unwitting part of us," as it is said. I think the same phrase can be applied to the church that has learned so much of which it is hardly aware during its long life with humankind. It is wiser than it knows; it has depths of understanding and a consciousness that has absorbed the symbols and myths of a hundred cultures. It knows more of the language of faith than it permits itself to speak; the church needs to believe more in its own creative capacity to bring forth new things and old from its treasure of human religious experience.

The black psychiatrist Franz Fanon once wrote that America should export poets rather than weapons and machinery to the developing countries of Africa. Commenting on this, psychologist Rollo May noted that this is because poets can communicate on a level that enables all men to recognize each other as brothers; when they can communicate in this way, they can also build community.

In the matter of believing, I think the church has poetic resources that it needs to free once more in behalf of the developing faith of humankind. This overflowing richness of the church's ability to hear and respond to the human search for faith is its prime resource; it has nothing to fear in believing that it can speak with meanings deeper than it knows itself. The church believes more than it believes literally, and history makes it urgent that it share all this with humankind rather than seal it away safe from the dangers of time, chance, and the questions of ordinary people.

In this second part of the book, I briefly attempt to integrate what I have learned while writing it and to share some of the things in which I truly believe. Having finished this book, I realize how much more there is to write on the subject; this is, then, a beginning, at best, but one that I hope will help others to look at and understand their own beliefs more fully.

Chapter One

Believing

"I believe in America." So begins what has become a powerful American myth. The suppliant, wax-mustached undertaker professes this as he presents his request for a favor to the godfather. He is a true believer in the classic and familiar mold, the patient and hopeful man who had come to a golden America, the fair land where things got better for immigrants from countries where things kept getting worse, the place in which one could invest belief because hard work and patience were ultimately rewarded. It is a worldly wise kind of belief, of course, one that is untroubled by its acceptance of evil in the nature of things. The little man believes in exchanged indebtedness, of pacts as ancient as the land he came from. He believes, most of all, in the godfather.

"I'd like to say I believe," intones the anguished celebrant in the *Mass* Leonard Bernstein composed in the same era in which Francis Ford Coppola created *The Godfather*. Bernstein gives us the plaintive intonation of a troubled and sensitive man, well educated but torn in his own conscience about the problem of believing. He is uncomfortable with the evil he cannot explain or do away with, and he cannot resolve the conflict that will not remain asleep within him.

He is far removed from the confident immigrant who puts his faith in the Mafia don.

He is more typical of modern people caught up in the profound anguish of wanting and needing to believe but uncertain of how to express or experience it. You can feel something dying in them as something else struggles for life, a search for that bridge that will bear them across the troubled waters of life.

These persons illustrate very differing aspects of our human need to believe. Belief has been looked on as something that helps us triumph over the natural, of virtue that strengthens us to assent to an explanatory system of truth. Because belief has come to seem a test of virtue, we have practically lost sight of how natural believing is for all humans. We are more familiar with the sudden willingness to believe in a God that is discovered in foxholes, a kind of belief long resisted but finally accepted by the repentant sinner. Believing has been the dramatic device pitting the person of religion against the person of science, the all or nothing kind of phenomenon that admitted little curiosity and few questions about its content. We may just be recovering from the notion of believing as a duty imposed by authority, one made ultimately more rewarding for us if we go along with it by banishing without examination all doubts and wonders.

It is hard for us to focus on believing as a healthy and quite normal human activity that always coexists with questioning and uncertainty. It is impossible for men and women to understand or fully humanize themselves without being believing persons. Too often the question of what they believe, especially if locked in literally interpreted language, obscures the essential role that active believing plays in their lives.

Furious battles have raged over what we should believe as well as about how and when we ought to believe. One does not necessarily make light of the content of belief by observing the number of pennants that have fluttered over the battlefields strewn with the corpses of believers at murderous odds with each other. Making war over beliefs is surely a sign of how important the activity of believing has always been to human beings; it is a tragedy, however, when this elementary human inclination is shriveled and scorched by the unknowing flames of controversy.

Forcing belief into the jaws of a vise contradicts what we understand about all other human functions. There is nothing locked in about the person, no way in which humans will ever hear or utter the last word on any issues in their lives. Believing will always retain notes of searching in healthy people who feel constrained and crippled if their spontaneous reflexes of belief are compromised by too many rigid or irreducible formulations.

The latter maneuvers are reactions of fearful and uncertain persons such as the archbishop of a great archdiocese who, with the urbanity and charm found in highly polished form among the successful Irish, once introduced me at a lecture series with premonitory observations about the accomplishments of the Second Vatican Council. Just before he ended his introduction, however, his voice grew quieter, as though his vocal cords sat tense in anticipation of the solemn words he was about to speak. He was a modern godfather, it seemed to me, reminding the family of how it functioned. "My dear people, you must remember that no matter how many fine speakers you hear, the bishops are the only true teachers in the Church."

This kind of remark has become almost a caricature for the administrative churchman who feels that orthodox beliefs are always in danger and must not be looked at too closely, much less tampered with. The same archbishop, in fact, told a distinguished gathering of biblical scholars that the best thing they could do was to gather together and recite the creed to themselves. This approach serves institutional but not personal ends. It may be very well for an organized church, for complicated reasons, to be very protective of what it classifies as the content of its beliefs.

That hide-the-treasure approach is frequently very hard, however, on believers urged to conform themselves to the demands made by the institution, even when these do not seem appropriate or helpful in their own lives. There is an inevitable tension between institution and individual that has been well recognized over the last generation in the Catholic Church. The essence of dialogue has consisted, to some extent, in that space where believers have tried to search out the full dimensions of their beliefs in the shadows of the institution that resists looking directly at them or honestly at its statements on faith.

It remains true, however, that persons must believe in order to be themselves. They are not inclined to disbelieve; they never reject religion arbitrarily. If we examine their struggles with belief we find that they are more often painful and difficult journeys rather than glib or prideful rejections of what the church terms its teaching authority. In a thousand ways men and women say, "I would like to say I believe." This has been their anguished cry throughout history as they have tried to understand and deepen their appreciation of the religious patterns and symbols they have been given to explain their lives.

Believing becomes more difficult as authority insists on precise requirements about the language, content, or conditions under which believing must be carried out, especially if these fail to capture the current cultural mood or reflect any reading of the beating pulse of human searchers. When these requirements, singly or in combination, fail to match people's unique visions of the world and their own experiences, they strike conflict as flints do flame.

Men and women are confused when this occurs because they find themselves suddenly in conflict with those they respect, their teachers, their priests, bishops, and even the pope, all the presumably trustworthy authorities who profess concern about them, their lives, and their salvation. Questing believers are made to feel pitted against tradition that seems to resist if not to repel their inquiries as improper. They are, after all, only experiencing the healthy human impulse to believe as deeply as they can.

More often than not, people's problems with religious faith arise not from an urge to disbelieve but from a passionate need to believe as richly and profoundly as possible. Men and women want to enter their lives as truthfully and deeply as possible, and they do not willingly put aside any system of teaching or any symbolic reference points that are more than the literal interpretations that serve only as STOP and GO signs.

Persons believe in something even when they style themselves as unbelievers. The latter word merely describes the fact that they can no longer accept certain styles of creed or that they cannot honestly respond to certain statements that are urged upon them as at the heart and core of God's revelation. They are saying that they cannot believe a certain, perhaps dated and no longer relevant formulation of faith; they are not saying that they cannot believe.

God has always been a problem for humans, not so much because of God but because of humans who have made believing into such a complicated process. To believe is, nonetheless, as essential for our survival and flourishing as air and water. Human beings need to believe and to expand their capacity to invest themselves in other persons, in causes, and in the religious concepts that allow them to take their places knowingly in the universe.

One of the earliest stages of our human growth, and one linked to the stable responsiveness of parents, is to develop a sense of trust in our environment, a reliance on the world we have entered to be constant in its responses, trustworthy so that, in a real sense, we know that we can count on it, that, in other words, we can believe in it. The primary agents of this are, of course, parents and, if they are inconsistent, absent, or otherwise fail to be trustworthy, reliable, or believable, they impair the capacity of the child to trust the world of human interaction, to be believers in trustworthy relationships. This impedes the child's ability to make friendships, relate to authorities such as teachers, and to be unguarded in believing in others or in God.

Believing is, then, an essential human function without which we cannot understand or integrate our personalities or pursue happiness in our lives and work. We should not be surprised to find that the phenomenon of believing, like all other human activity, can be snagged or frustrated, especially on or by the links of trust that are soldered indifferently or not at all by inconsistent or absent parents. We humans hunger to believe in order to touch and be touched by a constant universe, to feel alive emotionally even if we cannot understand the meaning of everything that happens in life; we want to believe because of the soundings of our own spirits that long for a world, a community, and other persons, as well as transcendent symbols on which we can depend. Our capacity for surrendering ourselves safely in love and fidelity to others depends on our first learning that the world and others are trustworthy. Our possibilities, our human destiny depends on our learning to believe.

We want to make some sense of our mostly unexceptional lives. Believing, with its past anchors and future referents, is not an easy task. Nor is it one that is ever completely finished; nonetheless, we are all engaged in it despite the diversity of our activities or our professions. Whether we think about our beliefs or state them explicitly and try to preach them to others, we operate from some surrounding patterns of interpretation that we learned early and through which we justify what we do in our lives.

The desire to believe, in other words, is everywhere to be observed even though its manifestations may seem irreligious or even antireligious at times. What is important to recognize is the essential humanity of this quest for at least partial understandings, handholds on, if not mastery of, existence, for some light as we make our way ever deeper into its mystery.

The evidence is not hard to discover. If there is one thing that young people articulate, it is their human longing, just like ours, to believe. They have been telling us that they are in need of credible adults, persons that they can believe in, older individuals who can provide models on which they can base their own lives. As will be discussed later, this pursuit of belief, sometimes awkward and ill stated, is a function of our making our way successfully into the trustworthy world through the trustworthiness of the people we believe in, those who raise us. Learning to believe, as flickering a longing as the matches they hold aloft like Mass candles at rock concerts, goes along with growing up.

The melancholy truth is that persons who have not developed some belief system to guide their lives have difficulty in maturing in all areas of their lives. It may well be that the content and style of a person's beliefs reflect, as well as anything else, the character of the development of his or her overall personality.

Some people say that they get by because they believe in music, while others believe in the gadgets falling literally from an Apple tree that inform them and allow them to communicate and that some seers think will lead to the *Singularity*, that turn in history when humans and machines finally merge with each other. Others check the polls, focus group opinions, statistics, or, God help them, what some celebrity says, to find something in which to believe.

All these, along with the Internet, which people can consult at any time for any opinion, have transformed ours into a new age of quasi-faith, of a negative's image not yet developed or printed on proper paper, of the need for and wonder of believing.

Information and scientific conclusions, after all, seem extraordinarily reliable, constantly interpreting and reinterpreting our lives just as horoscopes, tarot cards, and other devices out of history's dusty attic tell many what their lives mean or what choices they should make on matters ranging from the trivial to the sacred.

There may never have been a more rigidly orthodox set of beliefs than the tenets of psychoanalysis, a faith for many that has had its heretics and apostates as well as its true believers. Many presently believe in the movies, perhaps because the reproduction of life and sound in one of many available modes, from discs to DVRs, provides surrogate lives to some. It is not surprising to hear the veteran director Peter Bogdanovich, pale from a lack of sunshine, explain how he spends most of his time watching movies, especially those made before he was born. He is one of the many exegetes of American experience through the movies that constitute an environment of meaning and symbolism for them. Films are shown in temple-like surroundings, people travel like pilgrims to Lourdes to movie house shrines to make their way to the outer porch of the temple where concession stands, not unlike side altars in a cathedral, provide the elements needed for the sacrifice of two hours beneath the main altar, as big as St. Peter's, of the screen.

Films are celebrated at festivals, and often people say that seeing a real work of cinematic art is a religious experience. The artists of film are contemporary mythmakers, offering us the symbols that explore the conflicts and longings of their lives. This development carries a meaning for leaders of organized religion:

directors are doing the kind of work that they should be doing as they renew the eternal myths that fashion the truths about life, love, and death, which constitute the mystery of being alive. Do most movie directors know that they are doing this? No. Do most religious leaders know that they are not doing this? No, to the second question as well.

The task of religious leaders is not to be administrators, although they are chosen for their skills at that, but to be masters of the mythical symbols and stories that preserve, against the corrosive possibilities of time and chance, the believable spiritual significance of human life. The model for bishops in the future may not be the business administrators who balance books, but rather the artists who understand that their subjects are always essentially spiritual, always and ever about belief.

Great divergences exist among religious people, even within the same church. The Roman Catholic Church serves as the classic example. It makes room for people who believe in very different ways while at the same time, and for the institutional purposes mentioned before, it holds itself together against the shuddering impact of the varying styles of its believers.

Some Catholics believe persistently in miracles and a God who is somewhat stern and mindful of our slightest actions as He checks off our merits and demerits with the cold clear eye of a coach about to cut the team down to playing season size. Others see God as love and understanding, and are far more casual in the way they believe and in the way they worship. Still others are struggling somewhere in the middle, not sure exactly what they believe any more, but aware, at some level at least, that they have a very real need to believe in something in order to survive. The challenge for religious organizations to grasp and respond rather than to criticize exerts enormous pressure on them. It is not surprising that the Sheehan-Kobler study of American Catholic bishops done at Loyola University discovered that most bishops prefer paperwork to any other of their many activities.

There are those in life who believe in money or power, who profess a faith in bartering or buying what they conceive will be the most satisfying experiences of life. It may appear to be a sterile and isolating kind of belief system, one generally ill grasped by those motivated by it, but it marshals together great energies and is a pivot for powerful achievements.

For some, belief seems to be nothing but a memory, something mourned from an earlier period of life. Recollecting the time in which they put aside the only faith they ever knew, they say, as a well-known actor once did to me, "I don't have much to do with that stuff anymore." These people survive with a need to believe to which an adequate response has not been made; they have put away the childhood things, but nobody has given them the spiritual things of a true adult in which to believe.

Indeed, in Catholicism, a massive effort, termed "the Reform of the Reform" has, under the leadership of Popes John Paul II and Benedict XVI, sought to overturn the openness to the modern world that was a main achievement of Vatican Council II (1962–65) and lead believers back to an age in which the church rejected the world and preached in a simple and literal way the message of the scriptures, and spoke of morality in stark black and white terms.

Returning to an idealized past seems to give many people a solid, dependable sanctuary in which to stand, as the world of their childhood beliefs is riven with what seem to be earthquakes but are really the effects of mining the rich ore of faith that is found in the deepest recesses of their own personalities. People need new and more appropriate statements or images of faith to provide them with adult spiritual nourishment.

The traces of these previous beliefs, especially the echoes of the strong cultural setting in which they first heard them, are never erased from their memories. In this company, one may number sensitive people who feel that they cannot go home again to that glade of life in which such simple things were once so utterly believable. They are searchers, painfully aware of their need for something to believe in and frequently carrying with them, as Irish Catholic writers such as Eugene O'Neill, often do, the imprints they sometimes count as scars of long-gone beliefs that often become recurrent themes in their work.

Such individuals have not given up on believing; they would respond readily to those who might speak to them with suitable sophistication and understanding about their own questions and the surprisingly complex nature of life as they have known it. Frequently they have lost belief in the institution of the church because it seemed incapable of making room for them or of understanding their honest doubts about the beliefs it had urged at an earlier time and in a more literal fashion upon them.

The great mythologist Joseph Campbell had given up his Catholic practices when he realized through his studies that the versions of belief he had been taught were literal readings of biblical tales, such as the Garden of Eden, the Flood and Noah's ark, as well as other doctrinal articles, such as the Assumption, which were mythic in nature and whose meaning was therefore not literal but psychological and spiritual.

Campbell was greatly heartened by Vatican II's rediscovery and validation of approaches to the scriptures and theology that grasped their mythical character. An understanding of their mythical roots, as he said to me in many conversations, does not diminish but enhances the believer's faith. He always referred to Catholicism as "our Church" and asked for a priest on his death bed so that, as he put it, he could be reconciled with "the Church assembled."

Many people who have had good educations, if not the profound awareness of creative artists or scholars of myth, have come to question the ecclesiastical organization that has had such an influence on shaping the possibilities of their belief experiences. They know that religion has depths that cannot be grasped in the concrete religious language that, as we shall see, destroys rather than expresses the truths of faith. They are attracted, as Campbell understood, by theologians and others who help them to reinterpret certain religious statements or teachings, lest they be lost in archaic languages or styles of presentation that no longer speak to their present-day experiences or events.

At least some of these desire to believe, but they do not know quite what to believe in a time in which the Reform of the Reform seeks to lead them back into low-lying pastures of belief, easy to plow and harvest, after they have struggled on the journey to the Mount of Belief of which may be said what Saint John of the Cross said of the Mount of Perfection: "There is no way here," that is, no trail that has been cut and graded for easy travel to reach the heights of mature belief. Believing is not like reassembling a worn puzzle depicting a comforting scene of a cottage with a column of smoke rising above it as gently as an innocent child's prayer.

Such people can let go of such simple notions, grasping, when it is explained to them, that believers are not like the residents content with the routine of a retirement community. In fact, they are the Knights of the Round Table whose calling is to find the Grail of true belief. Like these knights, they must "enter the forest," as the myth tells us, "at its darkest part," that is, where nobody has hacked out a trail before them. Believing, like mourning, is hard work that no one else can do for us and that we must work on inside ourselves.

They cannot embark on this adult spiritual pilgrimage with old-fashioned maps that cannot be trusted for such a vital journey. These modern seekers can neither accept nor believe rigid authoritarian statements, and they often reluctantly conclude that this is what they get from the institutional church. Believing, for them, is a serious matter about which they are often surprised to discover that they possess deep and revealing emotions.

They do not want to stir the waters of faith that they perceive as muddy enough already. They do not want to push themselves to a point of unnecessary anguish or to an irrevocable decision against faith; and, longing for the revelation that a deeper analysis of creedal statements would offer, they live in some twilight where they can get a spurious security but not an integrated faith from accepting the old-fashioned protocols of the Reform of the Reform or while waiting for someone to open the richness rather than insist on the rigid literalness of the scriptures. Frustrated by catechism scraps of creedal articles that do not bring light to their lives, they can leave quietly rather than in noisy protest, sadly rather than happily as they search for an alternate faith that treats them as adults.

It is probably true that many arguments about faith are quite far removed from the ordinary individual's experience. While popes point in one direction, as if the creed were a succession of directional signs to be taken literally, and most theologians hesitate to accept the Reform of the Reform's rigid reinterpretation of Vatican II, these garden-variety believers are fully occupied in their day-to-day struggles to understand themselves, to raise their families, and to keep their marriages fresh; these challenges require them to plumb the mysteries of friendship and love, of suffering and loss, and to try to live purposefully in a difficult, painful, and conflicting world.

Perhaps believers need to be reintroduced to the process of believing as a natural, healthy, and quite resilient aspect of personality structure. The capacity to believe is intensely human. That is why it does not thrive when there is too much cement-hardened certainty or when no questions are allowed. Believing incorporates humans into life and into relationships with others in a manner that matches their inherent imperfections and incompleteness. Belief is necessarily a membrane stretched across our vulnerability, fragile even when it is strong. It is related to and depends on so many things that can shift or go wrong at almost any moment.

Believing is then a dynamic rather than a rigid quality. It expands and it contracts; it is more like breathing than holding one's breath. Believing cannot be activated by force or by fear. It arises from within us as a response to the situations, events, and symbols that we recognize as expressive of the truth of our lives; we believe in these when they adequately symbolize and match our experiences, when they help disclose not so much its concrete meaning as the presence of its unfathomable mystery to us.

Perhaps we should look at what supports us in our simple relationships and work to identify lynchpins of faith that support and integrate our experiences of existence. The latter may, at any given moment, seem fairly shaky; no one has ever seen God or been able to predict when or if death, illness, accident, or unexpected estrangement may smash the balance of our existences or surprise us with other experiences to test our beliefs.

Faith is conditioned by and is tied up at each step with the world and people as we know them; faith first has a simple operational definition and only secondly one that is theologically abstract. Believing becomes clearer as we recognize its thousand faces in our everyday lives. Believing is, in fact, what we live by.

The question of believing centers not on what dogmas we must accept or on what catechism answers we must accept unquestioningly from religious leaders. It is phrased far less dramatically but far more accurately this way: what do we believe in for ourselves, what beliefs have we made second nature to ourselves?

This is a hard question because it is much easier to recite the articles of a creed than it is to know and admit to ourselves just what it is that we count on or to identify the real foundations for the large and small decisions in our lives. We sometimes hesitate or actively resist exploring the true philosophy or theology with which we operate in our everyday lives.

Often believing is at best marginally related to the creed we recite on Sundays; it reveals to us, however, as nothing else does, our real human identities. Whether this is tentative or absolute, something mourned or something merely longed for, the mystery of believing is only understood when we uncover the truth of what we believe in ourselves.

Sometimes a kind of psychological archeology is needed to sift through the various deposits and artifacts that have piled up on this foundation during our lifetimes; at the bottom of the layers we come finally to a place where we can dig no deeper, where who we are and what we believe in, scraped clean of disguising debris, are laid bare at last.

Chapter Two

Believe It or Not:
The Language of Believing

The person can be defined as a believing phenomenon, as one who must believe in order to live at all. Believing is as fundamental as loving in the human situation, but few songs and little poetry are written about it. Sometimes it is only invoked publicly in the signs bobbing above the heads of fans at the Super Bowl or the World Series: "You've got to believe!" Really? That is more magical thinking than a profession of faith.

Believing, in such circumstances, and in organized religion as well, is a subject of relentless exhortation rather than celebration. You are free to love, but you must believe. Men and women have experienced such an imperative about belief that they have only slowly come to inspect it as their means of tapping into and freely symbolizing their identities and the meaning of their universe.

We speak casually of the fact that some things are easy while other things are hard to believe. That is not so much a statement about the relative truth of these objects of belief as it is a reflection of the psychological difficulties involved in committing oneself to a certain way of looking at the world. We speak in a similar way of people who have weak faith or strong faith; again we describe the inner states of the individuals rather than anything about the quality or even the character of what they believe. We have a limited vocabulary in which to discuss our subtle passion to believe; the inner urge and need to believe helps us recognize ourselves as human. For all our talk, we still only approximate an understanding of this essential human activity.

We have heard, for example, the traditional philosophical and theological approaches to the nature of belief, some of them magnificent in their explorations, within the possibilities of their own discipline, of human believing. Most of these reflections, however, are unavailable in any adequate translation for average persons. When helped to do so, they recognize that the language of belief is largely one of symbols and myths, poetic imagery that reaches, by routes they have not charted, into the deep layers of their beings.

The philosophical and theological analysis of faith is, for the average individual, too remote and frequently too dry to be helpful or satisfying. Despite the testimony it gives to the anguish of the researchers who produce it, academic faith generally remains abstract, afloat like a blimp above a bowl game over the everyday experience of humanity.

If you have ever heard a sermon preached by a philosophically minded clergyman to a relatively unsophisticated audience, you will appreciate the gulf that separates the trained mind (which might relish the reasoning involved) from the generally disinterested responses of the hearers who are absorbed with the simple complexities of living. It is not that they do not want to learn about their faith; rather they do not think about their experiences easily in the categories of philosophical or theological abstraction. Sometimes they cannot even recognize the faith they do possess when it comes in that form. Abstract talk about belief is just not the same as believing.

Most people understand that Sigmund Freud perceived religion as a neurotic outcropping from people's permanent senses of their own helplessness. Religion, in this view, is a regressive phenomenon that does not serve personal integration or in any way speak to the growth of personality. Many psychiatrists and theologians have rightly disagreed with this oversimplification, but it cannot be denied that this attitude has had a powerful effect on the estrangement of organized religion from the human sciences.

Freud clearly offered a belief system of his own; he felt that if persons recognized the unconscious origins of their own activities, they could be freed from the magical interpretations of the universe offered by the distorted religion he saw in his practice. This battle against traditional religion is not at an end despite the fact that many social scientists and psychiatrists have worked toward achieving a cease-fire and a measure of peaceful coexistence with theologians. Some scientists challenge this rapprochement vigorously, claiming in effect that the compromising social scientists are encouraging human beings to turn back toward an infantile interpretation of their world.

The social scientists of religion, chiefly anthropologists and sociologists, have provided brilliant analyses of the functional nature of believing in the history and life of humankind. They have not dealt with the essential nature of belief as much as with its sociological reality; they have observed in detail not only religion's persistence, but also a pervasive human need for religious interpretive systems in order to make life livable at all.

The symbol systems of religion, to risk a shorthand version of social science research, offer humans ways of looking at and comprehending their own existence and their activities, including those that are seemingly contradictory or inimical to them. The person is particularly fragile and dependent on effective symbols in order to interact with other persons and with the somewhat hostile universe.

Sociologist Robert Bellah's mid-twentieth-century message has not been improved on since he made it; humans must believe beyond belief that they must exercise their capacity to believe even when they cannot believe in the literal doctrines of their particular faiths. Believing, he says, is good for you no matter what you believe in. Believing is so essential, in this view, that it must be reinforced to prevent the structure of life as we know it to come unglued.

The research of social scientists reveals believing as a perennial function that is essential for the survival of men and women; without it, they will collapse in the face of life's inequities. These researchers have thrown a light on the deep roots of belief and have helped us to understand symbols and myths as essential food for believing persons. Indeed, social science research has refurbished the meaning of myth for modern persons, so they have come to appreciate anew that myths are not fables or deceptive stories.

The Native Tongue of Myth

Perhaps nothing had a greater impact on acquainting people with the rich meanings of myth than a television series hosted by Bill Moyers on the work of Joseph Campbell. Because of Campbell's influence, millions of believers have a better insight into myth and how it deepens rather than destroys their capacity to believe.

Religious myth is an enduring mode of communication through which essential notes about the human person are transmitted across the generations. Masters of mythology, such as Campbell, give us back the keys to the language of believing, an understanding of myths as bearers of the things humans dare not forget about themselves, including their ideals and the perennial conditions for their growth and development. Myths provide the symbols and stories in which we find and can identify our own stories and understand their significance.

Myth in Religious Tradition

As Campbell explained when I interviewed him for an article in the *New York Times Magazine* several years ago, "A mythology is an organization of symbolic images and narratives, metaphorical of the possibilities of human experience and the fulfillment of a given culture at a given time."

He noted that perhaps half the people in the world "believe that the metaphors of their religious tradition are facts. The other half do not believe they are facts at all." This, of course, sets up the false contest between faith and science, or between believers and atheists, that are so familiar to us even today. Scientists question the biblical version of creation while atheists reject, often with a seeming sense of superiority to believers, God as cruel, unfair, unjust, and woefully indifferent to human suffering.

So atheists, or those who have put away their childhood faith without finding adult faith to succeed it, scoff at the literal details of biblical faith, starting with the Garden of Eden, Adam and Eve, and the tempting serpent, and followed, like the credits at the end of a movie, by the large cast of biblical figures, crowd-scene extras, and special effects experts who provide the parting of the Red Sea, Noah's animal house of an ark surviving a great flood, and other wonders, from healing pools to stopping the sun's movement across the sky—the tales beyond number that fundamentalists, who believe in a literal reading of the Bible, accept as historical fact.

The literalists, for example, speak often of expeditions to find the wreckage of Noah's ark that they believe is still clutched by the overgrowth of some Middle Eastern mountain pass. Evidence of Noah's flodd is claimed by *Titanic* explorer, Robert Ballard.

Others seek the site of the actual Garden of Eden in the land we now call Iraq, certain that by the Euphrates a tree grew in a once-green paradise whose fruit our first parents were forbidden to eat. Had Adam and Eve resisted the tempting serpent, they believe, we would be living there in peace and abundance right now.

This situation, based on a misunderstanding of myth and its special language of metaphor, motivates many of the misunderstandings and almost all of the holy wars that have been waged in the name, not of true faith, but of a literalist misreading of the mytho-poetic language in which the Bible is written. Jihadists are Islamic fundamentalist believers in the Koran and its literal prescriptions.

Islam, we may note, speaks the same mythic language and, not surprisingly, has its own Garden of Eden, its story paralleling the narrative of Eden found in the Judeo-Christian tradition. In the Islamic version of the fall, the woman is punished with far more penalties than the exile, toil, and pain of childbirth that are brought against Eve. These stories are variants of the same myth whose point, as those of similar stories in other traditions, is not to explain the discovery of lust, as such Christian writers as Saint Augustine asserted, but to offer an explanation for the way we find ourselves, heirs of all the sorrows of the human condition, living in time rather than in eternity.

What Myths Do

Campbell explains the four traditional functions of myth: the first, he says, "is that of reconciling consciousness to the pre-conditions of its own existence—that is, of aligning waking consciousness of the *mysterium tremendum* of this universe, *as it is.*" Whether we think of "the world as it is, or the restoration of the world as it ought to be, the first function of mythology is *to arouse in the mind a sense of awe before that situation* through one of three ways of participating in it, *by moving out, moving in, or effecting a correction*" (emphasis added).

This, Campbell argues, "is the *essentially religious* function of mythology—that is, the mystical function, which represents the discovery and recognition of the dimension of the mystery of being."

The second function of mythology, according to Campbell, is "interpretive, to present a consistent image of the order of the cosmos." At about 3200 B.C., he explains, the idea of a cosmic order came into being "along with the notion that society and men and women should participate in that cosmic order because it is, in fact, the basic order of one's life."

Earlier than that, the focus of awe was not on the cosmic order but "on the extraordinary appearance of the animal that . . . seems to be particularly clever and bright, or on some striking aspect of the landscape. These predominate in the primitive world mythologies but something different enters as we attain consciousness of the 'great mysterious *tremendum* that manifests itself so impersonally that one cannot even pray to it, one can only be in awe of it.' The gods are merely agents of this mystery, 'the secret of which is found in mathematics.' "

As Campbell observes, "This can still be observed in our sciences in which the mathematics of time and space are regarded as the veil through which the great mystery, the *tremendum*, manifests itself," that science, of course, reflected the understandings achieved at various times in history so it should not surprise us that the Bible reflects "the cosmology of the third millennium, B.C."

Here Campbell injects a note critical to our understanding the scriptures that undergird faith: "Those who do not understand the metaphor, the language of religious revelation, find themselves up against the images that they accept or contest as facts." On that shore of nonliteral images struck to herald the *tremendum*, fundamentalists find themselves stranded, as shipwrecked sailors might be as they behold the massive silent gods on Easter Island. The latter hint at the mystery of the *tremendum*; they do not, in themselves, constitute the mystery.

The third function of myth is, according to Campbell, "to validate and support a specific moral order, that order of the society out of which they arose." Mythology therefore "reinforces the moral order by shaping the person to the specific demands of a specific geographically and historically conditioned social group." Rites of initiation, some of which are quite brutal in the ritual testing involved in making the young cross the threshold from childhood into adulthood, are classic examples of this.

These rituals include "scarification and certain minor surgeries . . . carried out so that persons could realize that they no longer had the same body they had as children." These socially ordered rituals "were to incorporate them, mind and body, into a larger, more enduring cultural body whose explanatory mythology becomes its own." It is critical to note the shift here to a force of society instead of nature.

So, in India, social authority kept the caste system in place along with the rituals and mythology of suttee. That, as we note about Western institutional religion, is the point of risk for the institution when it forces on people, as Campbell expresses it, "mythological structures that no longer match their human experience."

When this happens, as, for example, in churches that teach that sexual relations outside of marriage are always mortally sinful, the process of "mythic dissociation" occurs. Through the latter, Campbell explains, "persons reject or are cut off from explanatory notions about the order of their lives."

They are then the shipwrecked mariners blinking open their eyes on an Easter Island beach to stare into the stone idol eyes of gigantic figures that, for these survivors of the sea, cannot be and are not gods, revelations of the mystery of the *tremendum,* or, finally, the source of a believable moral code.

This is the danger for the Catholic Church when its leaders attempt, as Pope Benedict XVI does in his Reform of the Reform, to refurbish as literal, the myths, rituals, and concrete scriptural readings of a bygone time. Many people find that these no longer match their human experiences and therefore cannot accept them or the parts of the moral order that they are supposed to support. At times human experience, especially in areas of sexuality, is far ahead of the moral reflection that a large bureaucratically top-heavy institution must carry out to offer moral insights on evolving moral issues. The organization tends to reinforce itself by insisting on the literal meaning of its mythological treasures and, thinking that it is keeping the faith, is actually damaging it, diluting and diffusing its teaching power even as it insists on its own teaching authority.

The fourth function of mythology is to support "the individual through the various stages and crises of life—that is, to help persons grasp the unfolding of life with integrity."

That means that mythology, or, as we may say, the faith, the believing, if you will, taught by the church, is ordered to the significant events of human life. The effective mythology of its teachings should help persons live "in accord with, first, themselves, and, secondly, with their culture, as well as the universe, and, lastly, with that *mysterium tremendum* beyond themselves and all things." This is realized in the church's pastoral understanding, the signature of Vatican II's renewal.

Keeping up with the Mythic Language of Believing: Understanding Metaphor

The recognition that myth is the language of believing has enabled scripture scholars to reinvestigate the Bible and to tell again its magnificent stories without the penalty of the literalness that makes believing increasingly difficult for educated and scientific minds. This demythologization of the scriptures has had extensive reverberations in theology and, more recently, in the ordinary life of Christians who, frequently without much preparation, have suddenly seen and heard their familiar faith myths laid open for them in a fresh and reinvigorating way.

We cannot appreciate this language without understanding metaphor, the language in which the scriptures are written. Metaphor comes from *meta* meaning *over, across,* and *pherein* meaning *to carry, to bear.* A metaphor carries us, bears us, allows us to make a journey that we could not otherwise make. As Campbell notes, metaphors "deliver more than just an intellectual concept, for such is their inner character that they provide a sense of actual participation in a realization of transference. The symbol, energized by metaphor, conveys, not just an idea of the infinite but some realization of the infinite." The metaphor bears you across the barriers of specific times and places to experience that which is beyond them that can only be reached through metaphor.

Metaphors are rich in their connotations. That makes them different from concrete words, such as STOP signs, that possess only a denotation. When the metaphorical language of the scriptures is read as literally as a traffic sign, that is, accepted only in its denotation, then its connotations are sheared away, and the journey beyond the literal to the transcendent is frustrated.

This happens to the language of believing whenever the metaphorical language of the scriptures is taken literally, that is, in a localized, culturally specific way that leaves us only with the denotation, the treasure chest without the treasure, that is, a concrete, literal understanding, a downed line that does not carry the illuminating richness of the connotations that allow us to experience transcendence.

Believers may feel that they have achieved a level of certainty that they can count on when they take religious language literally, but they also sacrifice the deeper religious, transcendent meaning at the same time. Literal meaning is a hardtack ration compared to the rich feast of the metaphors that energize the myths that open us to mystery. It resembles, as Campbell once expressed it, "ordering your lunch and eating the menu."

An Example

In the Catholic Church, dogmatic teachings are often based on concrete renderings of a spiritual language, as, for example, in the dogma of the Assumption of the Blessed Mother into Heaven, which was declared a dogma of the faith by Pope Pius XII in 1950. The dogma's literal meaning is that the body of Mary lifted off from the earth and traveled upward directly to a heaven that we locate imaginatively beyond the skyscape.

At the time, Graham Greene wrote an essay in *LIFE* magazine suggesting that the significance of this literal understanding lay in its underscoring the value of the individual person in an age of the Holocaust's mass murder, Hiroshima and Nagasaki, and the deaths beyond counting of two world wars. Psychologist Carl Jung, however, viewed the Assumption as a metaphor, that is, a rich symbol of transcendence, of a mystery deeper than that of the literal connections that Greene had sensed.

The Assumption, declared at the very middle of the century that would usher in the Space/Information Age, was, for Jung, a symbol of Mother Earth returning to the heavens, a metaphor rich in connotations not only about the person, but about the healing of the rift between heaven and earth and therefore the separation of body and soul that had undergirded so much literal and limiting theology. Believing is not destroyed but enlarged and deepened by this expansive insight into the metaphorical meaning of the Assumption.

The literal meaning was based on an outdated and irrelevant cosmology that was developed 4,000 years B.C. by priests, in the land known now as Iraq, when they observed the passage of planets through fixed stars. They imagined a universal order with the earth and the heavens divided, with the earth below and the heavens above. This gave rise both to astronomy and astrology, the latter pairing events on earth with those in the heavens.

This concept of a divided universe was the basis for the hierarchical ordering of that universe and of the human person. The person was divided into the soul that was good and the body that was bad; the intellect was set against the emotions, all these false divisions forced into a template that was pressed down, firmly and falsely, on human personality.

The human community was also divided into a hierarchical display in which the most worthy were placed at the top and the least worthy were exiled to the bottom. This way of looking at the person, the community, and the universe made their division into grades of worthiness seem natural as if God had made things this way.

This ancient stained glass image, misshapen by its bubbled and distorted surface, was shattered by the advent of the Space/Information Age that restored a sense of unity to the universe and to the human person. The Assumption symbolizes the healing of that wound in the cosmos for Mother Earth did return to the heavens in the Space/Information Age. When humans left footprints on the moon's dusty surface, they also made it possible for all of us, through television, to view the first image of earthrise and to see for ourselves that the earth is not *divided from* the heavens but is *in* the heavens. The Assumption, as the literal transport of the virgin's body into a place above where we locate a literally laid out heaven, is an impoverished image whose denotation deprives us of grasping the great mystery revealed in the metaphor.

Metaphor Lighting Religious Mystery from Within

Campbell felt that people were denied participation in the *Mysterium Tremendum et Fascinans* by the reduction of religious language to ethnically localized denotations, as though the latter expressed actual historical events rather than served as routes to the transcendent.

He speaks, for example, of the virgin birth, noting that this metaphor "has been presented as an historical fact, fashioned into a concrete article of faith over which theologians have argued for hundreds of years, often with grave and disruptive consequences. Practically every mythology in the world has used this 'elementary' or co-natural idea of a virgin birth to refer to a spiritual rather than an historical reality." Its connotation is to a wondrous event, to a transcendent experience available spiritually to all. We can all experience a virgin birth of the spirit.

So, too, of the metaphor of the Promised Land, "which," as Campbell notes, "in its denotation plots nothing but a piece of earthly geography to be taken by force. Its connotation—that is, its real meaning—however, is of a spiritual place in the heart that can only be entered by contemplation."

Perhaps the most overused and misunderstood metaphor is that of the End of the World, that, taken literally as it is by fundamentalists and others who try to calculate it from misreading the scriptures as history and who are constantly scheduling and rescheduling it, refers to a cataclysmic fiery end of the world. That is the denotation of the phrase.

The connotation—the spiritual meaning—is much deeper and allows us to make a journey we could not otherwise make into mystery. The End of the World refers to something that happens every time that we see more deeply into its wonder. Then, the world we know comes to an end and we enter another that is spiritually richer for us. This follows the mystical poet Blake's invitation "to cleanse the doors of perception and to see the world as it is, infinite." The metaphor is not meant to frighten but to open believers to a deeper reality, to give them something truly transcendent and nourishing in which to believe.

As Campbell concludes, "These images must point past all meanings given, beyond all definitions and relationships, to that really ineffable mystery that is just the existence, the being of ourselves, and this world. If you give that mystery an exact meaning we diminish the experience of its own depth . . . here we sense the function of metaphor that allows us to make a journey we could not otherwise make, past all categories of definition."

The restorationist impulse of the papally led movement known as the Reform of the Reform, like eighteenth-century efforts to restore France's monarchy, wants to return to an ordering of the universe and a translation of its language that does not fit the modern day or match the experiences of ordinary people. The dominant motif, on clear display in the revised language of the Mass imposed on Catholics in 2011, is to accept the restrictive *literal* rather than the expansive *mythological* nature of the language of revelation.

The living language of poetry has been presented again to believers as the proper language of faith. The old historical and narrow interpretation has been revived in the Reform of the Reform. This is an effort to halt the revolution in teaching and understanding the content and meaning of faith, which advances in a theological grasp and use of the language of believing. The Reform of the Reform, perhaps unintentionally, may generate a new crisis that pits official insistence on reviving the literal meaning of scripture against the rich harvest of transcendent understanding that is the yield of reclaiming the mytho-poetic depths of religious language.

This enterprise is by no means concluded, and the practical effects of restaging the epical themes of man's beliefs in modern times continue to cause anguish, disappointment, and disillusionment in those persons who have been instructed in a rigid interpretation of historical faith. The conflict between the literalists who now prevail and those striving to preserve the updated appreciation of the mythical language of believing is the little-publicized but greatest challenge to the Catholic Church in the second decade of the twenty-first century.

In other words, in great numbers, persons have reclaimed a feeling for the essentially human intuitive processes through which religious truths have been preserved in our consciousness throughout history. There exist, it would seem, spiritual capacities in human beings that stir into wakefulness without elaborate instruction in the presence of profound symbols and myths.

This is not basically a rational process, and it can neither be planned nor activated by intellectual means or mathematical procedures. The great souls of each century hear the new music that sings again of the basic materials of belief; they respond to it and, without quite knowing what they are doing, they help us to understand it through the symbols—artistic, cinematic, liturgical—that they fashion for us.

These responsive souls are always processing the experience at the borders of our awareness and, like good leaders, calling back to us so that we can follow them forward. It is difficult to recapture a sense of the poetic as the language of faith precisely because the unpoetic are once more reviving their preferences for expressing faith in hard and fast literal creedal statements. They are offering us the cardboard menu instead of the nourishing meal.

They try, in effect, to flash freeze isolated moments in the long story of human awareness and to mark these off as the approved and sacred quadrants of belief. This has proved not only deadly to poets but to belief and the act of believing as well. It is one of the reasons that the pope sponsoring this restoration ends up, surely against his intention, distancing himself from the human experience whose transcendent nature it is his calling to illuminate.

This is not to say that faith is irrational; it is, however, necessary to recognize that it is a response of the total person and that, as such, it has always expressed itself best in the most abiding personal language we know, that of myth and poetry. That is the only language supple enough to express the *Mysterium Tremendum et Fascinans* (the great and gripping mystery) of being alive just as we are in the world just as it is. Defining a profound religious truth in the exact language of any one age may diminish rather than enhance its spiritual meaning, leaving it vulnerable to the decay and death of concrete languages.

Mytho-poetic language protects spiritual truth, allowing it to flow in its original purity and power through the narrowed canyons and steep gorges of passing time. Faith renews itself in this water, the symbol of the ineffable and of the unconscious that flows through the scriptures. The Jews enter Egypt through Joseph in the water source of the well; they leave through the parted seas.

These are not to be understood as literal stories but, as we have noted, mythic accounts of fundamental spiritual and psychological truths about human beings and human existence. Faith may be understood as the sense of believers, the way of looking at and inserting themselves into life, always expressed in poetic ways that protect their underlining of the transcendent moments of life from the effects of time and chance that shrivel literal religion as a bright flame does a brittle parchment.

The decline of dogma may be related to the contemporary person's rejection of nonmythic categories far more than a rejection of believing. It is clear that the rediscovery of the special language of belief leaves many people unsatisfied by the literal approach to faith. Still, the Reform of the Reform, led by Pope Benedict XVI, plays upon the longing many people have for a faith that excludes ambiguity and delivers religion straight up, as clear and bracing as a martini. That makes religion the cocktail rather than the opium of the people. It is the brew offered to the good ordinary people who have been taught that religion is principally something to hold onto, a life preserver of faith that has a simple purpose: to keep them afloat in dangerous seas.

But as a people we have been so constrained poetically that we are only beginning to sensitize ourselves to its special communication—and we do not yet fully recognize the signs and symbols that are already present all around us, making our world "transparent," in Campbell's phrase, "to transcendence," allowing us to experience the end of the world every day with the terror removed and the wonder restored. These symbols are being rediscovered and refurbished by the contemporary poets of faith who function in the arts and even in contemporary theological studies—and who will teach again this glorious language to believers.

We live in a period of waiting, in which worn-down literalism will not, in the long run, speak to believers but in which new symbols and poetry, appropriate for the Space/Information Age wait to be fully recognized and incorporated into the life of the church and other institutions.

When literal biblical beliefs can no longer be accepted without question, humans experience the spiritual hunger that arises from what is termed "myth deprivation." This state may be read in the renewed interest in the occult as well as in the enlarged focus in movies and television on vampires, zombies, and paranormal phenomena. Psychiatrists have speculated that the widespread interest in the occult resembles the irrational and sometimes psychotic—like behavior of individuals who are deprived of their dreams in the course of sleep research. It has been noted that if experimental subjects are awakened just as they begin to dream—if, in other words, their dreams are denied them—they suffer from this loss in very obvious ways.

Dreams can be merely the leavings of the day's experiences, a processing of what psychiatrists term "day residue." But they can also hold greater and richer significance than being a kind of maid service for our personalities. They can be more than random representations and instead provide the chronicles or projections of the dynamic inner myth that attempts to integrate symbolically the way we inhabit our existence.

Dreams do this in a semipoetic fashion, using symbolism and condensation as well as exaggeration in dealing with the day's events. We seem to need this dream activity during our sleeping hours in order to preserve our personalities in an adjusted and healthy state. Psychiatrists suggest that people analogously need well-developed myths for this very same reason: they have been denied the integration of self that is provided by the waking dreams of myth.

Men and women need this mythic kind of vision in order to keep themselves together, in order to maintain their adjustments, and to define themselves accurately in space and time. They serve the function of the faith that makes us whole.

Believing has also been observed in the medical and educational institutions of the world. It is no secret that faith that is alive, the activated capacity to believe in one's self and in one's future, is decisive for the health and growth of the person. This has been demonstrated many times in careful research on the role of believing in physical and psychological illness. Belief is at least as powerful as any known medication, but it is still one that is not understood very well. Its magic is found only by passing through the always open portal of myth

All we know, as psychiatrist Jerome B. Frank expressed in his classic *Persuasion and Healing*, is that there is a dynamic associated with believing in other persons that transforms their chances, reversing the odds in desperate situations and frequently making the difference between life and death. This has also been observed in education and in many other parts of life where the role of expectation—of an active optimistic belief in the potential of other individuals—does, in fact, enable them to achieve performances beyond those that might, on other grounds, have been predicted for them. Believing is powerful medicine just as the failure to believe—the withholding of the investment of the self—is a negative and destructive force.

Believing is, then, central to understanding humans, as vital to them as anything we know. Persons believe with all of themselves, and they recognize and respond without effort to those who can speak faith's special language to them. We need to believe appropriately in the institutions that are meant to preserve and share the faith but not with the blind loyalty that kills believing altogether.

We are just not ourselves unless we believe and are believed in; that is the abiding wonder of living faith. Loyalty is not the same as faith, although a lot of ecclesiastics would like you to think so. We need a living faith through which the ecclesiastical institution will open itself more fully to its own poetic energies and be able to hear and speak the language of believing more clearly. Jesus told his disciples that they were called to speak "entirely new languages."

The "gift of tongues" is not some mysterious, Berlitz-like capacity to speak German, French, and Arabic to various hearers, but to understand and to use effectively the language that speaks of believing in a truly human way. The institutional churches have a struggle on their hands, but it is not to quell a riot or a rebellion, as Pope Benedict XVI characterized the transition after Vatican II. It lies rather in reclaiming its mytho-poetic language and, by speaking it, to give humans something rich and deep enough in which to believe.

We may not be able to measure these transactions very well yet, but we can recognize them when they occur. When we do not believe in somebody, we have already taken away something of their chances for finding or becoming themselves. Teachers can do this to their students, coaches with their athletes, and priests to their people. Believing is not magic. It is profoundly human, a source of energy and self-integration, the like of which is not observed in any other aspect of human experience. In questions of growth, human relationships, and healthy achievement, the role of believing is crucial. It is faith, an active kind of believing, which makes men and women whole.

Believing is a sensitive aspect of human experience, and myth is the extraordinary medium through which humans deal with the complexities and search for purpose in their waking hours; if they are deprived of them, they will emit disturbing behaviors similar to those observed in individuals deprived of the symbolic processing of the dreams that integrate the seemingly piecemeal stimuli of everyday life.

Myth serves the believing person; it is not a romantic and irrelevant occurrence any more than dreaming is. Humans need something more than hard facts and numbers in order to understand their lives. They cannot be real, in other words, unless they have positive myths available to them; they need the language of myth to be able to believe; they need essential beliefs spoken in mythic language in order to live.

Institutions and Believing

Believing, however, must also be understood as a social phenomenon, and the persons learn to believe best in a community of the faithful who provide the human setting for it. Believing is better than it is made to seem by institutional churches that so slowly and cautiously expose themselves to new ideas about it; it is more lively than it seems in organizations so set on maintaining their own adjustment and stability and ignoring their opportunities for service to believing persons.

It is not surprising to find institutions, such as organized churches, somewhat hesitant to accept and incorporate these new insights into the proclamation of old beliefs. There is an inertia in all institutions that is quite natural. They cannot be as responsive to changing situations as human beings, and it is a long and nearly miraculous process when institutions can at last absorb and make use of what the poets tell them about the world. That they manage to do it at all is the extraordinary thing.

That is why the churches have always needed prophets, perhaps beating their breasts or speaking in a difficult language or behaving incomprehensibly as teachers, as processors of reality who attune the churches to the changing moods and needs of history. It is not surprising that institutions, which seek necessarily to maintain stability, hardly ever enthusiastically endorse new developments either in theology or in science. They wait, as time has taught them to, and often much longer than they need to, before they open themselves in an unguarded way to new learning.

The institutional churches have always run the risk of making themselves unbelievable in the problems they have manifested in speaking about the nature of believing. In fact, many churches have spoken in rather sure and absolute terms about this subject, which cannot be discussed in this fashion very intelligibly at all. They have been quick to insist on their authority and their right to define and defend specific beliefs, but these stances have usually frustrated genuine religious searchers and moved genuine prophets to despair.

When an institution is sluggish, when authority shows little sign of being able to seek, in due time, better constructs in which to speak about beliefs, then believers turn their gazes elsewhere, looking for those who can speak to their experiences and to their need to believe. An institution that has not completely lost its sensitivity to new language and new concepts is vital to the informed tasks of believing or of sharing beliefs with the men and women of its time. That is why the Jesuit historian John O'Malley writes in "What Happened at Vatican II?" that the Council was primarily a "language event."

When institutions hold on to outmoded categories and symbols, they cease speaking the language of believing altogether. And it is very hard for them to surrender these because, when they emphasize the literal, as Pope Benedict XVI does in his Reform of the Reform, such institutions believe that by surrendering their enshrinement of the literal, they surrender the faith itself. They have overidentified concrete ways of speaking of the faith with the idea of believing itself.

It is this process, so endemic to institutions, that makes them seem perennially irrelevant to the world in which they live. When any church shows signs of stirring, as the Roman Catholic Church did in Vatican Council II, the response to its efforts is enormous. When it slumps back, made fearful by its own initiatives, it causes the kind of disappointment that can only be known by people who truly want to believe and who sense that perhaps this institution, despite its encrustations, could still speak the vital words of life to the pain-ridden world. Lose a feeling for the language of believing and you lose a sense of the dynamic meaning of believing.

One practical conclusion, of course, is not to make belief that sole possession of institutions, although institutions are obviously critically important for a community of believers. One must not expect institutions to surmount their inherent difficulties any more swiftly than any of us do. That is what lies beneath the present effort to take the church back to a seemingly simpler time when the creed was accepted, article by article, as the true and final expression of belief.

While this is tragically misguided in its backward thrust, it is understandable that even a theologically well-trained pope may have difficulty in moving into a truly new age. Perhaps we should learn to believe appropriately in institutions like the church, not so much with a grain of salt as with a measure of compassion and understanding for the awkwardness and difficulty with which it must necessarily move through history.

Indeed, the wonder is that it moves at all; believe in the institutional church as it is, but that excludes instantaneous miracles from the organizational housing that can never quite catch up with the world around it. The danger with institutions is to overbelieve in them, to commit oneself beyond what is appropriate or even reasonable, in a blind and naïve loyalty that takes the name of faith even when it is only distantly related to it.

All these signal the human need for the nourishment of mythic understanding to keep their belief alive. Believers long not to be delivered from faith but to be nourished by the richness of a faith whose metaphorically rich myths render their daily worlds, in the words of Joseph Campbell that also express the sacramental mission of the church, "transparent to transcendence."

Chapter Three

Inside Belief

In a very real sense, all of us make our own worlds. Not one of us is completely passive to any of the experiences we have in life. We actively fashion these, or we would be strangers to invention and learning as well as to real love. Something of us has to get into these, or they would not exist at all. The role of knowers, the philosophers tell us, is crucial to the character of the knowledge they acquire. The inner states of the lover, as psychological research informs us, define the truth or falsity of the friendship in which he or she is a partner.

The same reciprocal dynamic applies to believers; they cannot be thought of as merely passive to the gifts of faith; they are, in fact, integral parts of the believing response itself. Without an understanding of the active role of believers, there can be no understanding of belief at all.

An appreciation of believing demands a redefinition of faith as the living positive response of the believer; it is strongly dependent upon and conditioned by the believer's general psychological readiness for this. Faith does not float freely in an engulfing supernatural atmosphere; the human element is strongly determinative.

Faith is faulted hopelessly when it is conceived of in an extrinsic or static fashion. It is not a possession in the manner of an inert object that, no matter how much we cherish it, can never become a part of ourselves. Faith is not born outside of us; nor does it take its strength and significance from a distant sphere that is defined over human awareness and human experience.

The charge that any view of faith that relates it too intimately to the personality of a human being is excessively naturalistic is indeed familiar. It echoes a divided model of the universe and of the person that in the Space/Information Age can no longer profitably be employed in discussing a subject as sensitive as religious faith and belief. To suggest that faith is generated in the heart of human personality and that it parallels its course of growth is to stand in true wonder at God's grandeur.

The effort to make faith some kind of objective entity, capriciously given or withheld and haphazardly earned or lost, has made it more, rather than less, difficult to understand the believing nature of humans. Living faith can only be seen in living persons; it demands that we observe the slow and humanly conditioned process through which our capacity to believe is activated. Believing is influenced, as is our perception of the world, by our inner states in relationship to external sources of stimulation.

Many factors combine their influence in forming the texture of this faith-perception of the universe. A close look at the person shows that faith is not a simple notion, like the image of the totally natural man flooded by rays of grace coming down from heaven. Indeed, as we proceed in our understanding of faith, we enter into depths of human individuality previously untapped and frequently unrecognized.

There exists, in other words, a nonrational dimension to the faith response that radiates from layers of human experience to which rational language is a stranger. These dynamic facets of personality are powerfully influential in shaping our understanding of our world; and in and through them, we learn meanings of life that we never quite put into words but nonetheless know. At this level of human experience, we appreciate the need for myths and symbols as an ancient but always fresh and necessary language of human personality. Faith lives at this level in each one of us.

As we have retired the model of a divided universe with the advent of the age of science and space flight, so too we are forced to put aside the model of the divided person that was necessary to sustain older concepts of faith as static distinguished from ourselves and our own human unity. Faith is closely linked to the person, a living quality as pervasive and real as the person's spirit and similarly related to our total human identity.

There is no believing that does not involve the whole person. You cannot give the response of faith with only a part of your personality. This would be to contradict and to diminish the fullness of the stance we are required to take through any profession of personal faith. Faith comes from the whole us, or it is not faith at all.

Believing has rational elements, of course, but its energies run through our sinews and unconscious pathways, through all the aspects of our personality to which insufficient attention has previously been paid. This has not necessarily been a difficulty for ordinary persons who, unhobbled by excessively rational analysis or self-consciousness, often feel belief as a deep and organizing part of themselves, something of the heart as well as the mind. That is why people have always responded to effective symbols of belief— because they could understand and respond to that language even if they could not parse it.

Faith involves struggle, an effort to sense the fullness of ourselves at the moment we commit ourselves in belief. And to believe is essential to the activation and coordination of all the processes through which we reach toward our own individuality and fullness.

Believing is related to the complex human process we call growth; its character is keyed to the total development of ourselves.

There is something fundamental about believing that transcends any specific categories of creed or other intellectual statements of beliefs. It is, as growth is more than rational statements concerning life, much more than that. As Paul Tillich has observed, "Faith in the biblical view, is an act of . . . the whole personality. Will, knowledge, and emotion participate in it. It is an act of self-surrender, of obedience, of assent. Each of these elements must be present."

Believing cannot, then, be separated from the personalities of believers. To believe fully is proof that we are there, that the elements of our identity cohere, that we have a sense of ourselves we can invest in something outside of ourselves. I believe, we might say, therefore, I am. Through every act of believing we are, in fact, born again spiritually. We experience what is mythologically described as a virgin birth.

So too, believing is subject to the approximately understood laws of development that regulate all the other aspects of human growth. Believing does not live above and beyond the growing personality; it does not possess a fully mature mode of being independent of the individual's general personal development. Believing is a positive capacity that is fed by and, like a river gathering strength from collateral streams, in turn, feeds human experience.

Faith is so tied up with our growing that it is notably affected, from infancy onward, by the relationships that are significant in the individual's life. This environment of human beings is exactly right to actuate all our capacities, including that of believing.

In the development of faith, we note the gathering together of some of the most basic and prized signatures of human experience. These include, as Professor Thomas A. Droege long ago observed, trust, obedience, knowledge, assent, commitment, and centeredness.

All these ultimately demand an investment of the whole person. As the individual man or woman grows, the meaning and quality of these experiences shift, and one may become more important than the other; although never totally independent of each other, they may be stressed differently at various points on the curve of development.

The origins of our capacity to believe lie in our earliest experience when, in helplessness and without words, we begin to sense the world as believable or not. We possess the latent possibilities of believing, but whether and to what extent we exercise these depends on the reactions of those persons closest to us.

We should not, of course, be surprised by the idea of faith as a component of personality shaped by interpersonal experience. Jesus seems to speak of it this way in the Gospels, pointing to little children for an understanding of the meaning of believing. He did not mean merely to underscore them as models of trust and openness; sometimes children are not like that at all.

Instead, Jesus' comparison suggests also the human context in which children grow and develop into mature believers. This movement depends on the manner in which their beginning faith is greeted by the believers who bring them up.

The quality of believing that we experience from others in our earliest development is a crucial determinant of the style of belief of which we are then capable. Whether we believe hinges on whether we are believed in. It is interesting to recall the nature of the authority that parents exercise over children. It springs from their relationship, because they are the authors of the children, and not from some extrinsic set of rules. It is a relationship that takes on its meaning from the special relationship of the human beings involved in it. This is a totally different order of experience from that of politics, manipulation, or impersonal power.

The existence and health of the authority of parents depends on their capacity to stay in relationship—and to change the relationship appropriately—with their growing children. This kind of authority speaks to us of the original meaning of the word "to make able to grow." The development of faith falls into this order of experience too. It is calibrated to interpersonal realities, to those near mysterious transactions between people that cannot be faked and that cannot be claimed to exist when, in fact, they do not. Faith depends on a reality like friendship rather than a rule of law. As a human capacity, believing is energized only by other humans who actually believe in us.

This makes it all the more regrettable that faith has been treated as something responsive to the commands of power by some ecclesiastics. Faith has never grown because of force or manipulation; genuine faith has, in fact, always been stronger than these exercises of power. It is obviously not very helpful to instruct people in belief through threats of present or imminent punishments.

People may well give some kind of assent to religious formulas under this pressure, but it is never true faith. In the same way, it is obvious that those persons who help people to find or to rediscover their faith are profoundly human believers themselves. Pope John XXIII is a well-known example of this, a believing pastor whose authority lay not in power but in love. He made believing easier for human beings.

It is proper to ask, in this context, whether we can find any difference, or whether we should presume that any would exist, in the basic character of our believing response toward God and toward each other. It is difficult to imagine that some other activity, alien but superior to our human belief capacity, is required in order to have faith in God. Once again the statements of Jesus are instructive. His invitation is to "believe in me," a statement that cannot possibly be grasped by anyone who does not know something about friendship and love.

Faith language is human language, after all, and if friendship with God does not have a human face, then it is beyond us completely. We return to the human person to understand anything and everything about faith in God. This is the message and the incarnation, but in a world where some theologies still insist on a kind of dread or a terror before the awesome face of God, we may forget that believing is a human activity, part of what God gave us to respond to each other and to Him.

We believe best, not when we escape our human condition, but when we are at ease and untroubled about it. Openness to God is mediated always by our human condition. Faith is a living filament threaded through all our existence, and as we trace this through the personal relationships through which we have learned to believe, we join ourselves to the mystery of believing in someone beyond us.

It is unfortunately true that the institutional concern for orthodoxy has often been more properly a concern to maintain religious authority and control. When this authority is not conceived of as a living experience, it cannot vitalize faith, although it may fix it in static statements of belief and create an illusion of security. Believing in any human context never grows deeper merely because of security. Believing lives in a more perilous and contingent world, not in some maximum security ecclesiastical Fort Knox.

Faith, in fact, is uneasy with too much security; what, indeed, could faith mean in a totally predictable world? Churchpeople who worry too much about the loss of faith may never have learned to believe themselves. It is not an exaggeration to suggest that many prelates who seem quite anxious about what others believe in do not seem to believe much in their people. So, too, contemporary parents who are excessively upset about their

children's attitudes toward religion may be telling us about their
own shaky faith.

They find it difficult to communicate faith because they conceive of it too exclusively in terms of duty rather than as a living
testimony to God's existence and goodness to us. Religion is always
given a bad name, and faith seems like a soggy burden when it is
urged by people who do not believe fundamentally in the capacity
of other people at all. These people shield themselves from others
and thus make themselves unbelievable. Nothing is emptier than
sermons of faith in God preached by clergy who cannot believe in
persons. Unbelieving ritual gestures made in the name of such faith
are the original obscene gestures.

The fundamental faith-shaping experiences of infants is associated
with their developing senses of trust, perceptions of the world as a
friendly and reliable place in which people intend to do them good
rather than harm. This, according to psychoanalyst Erik Erikson, is
the work of the first year of life and the responsibility and opportunity of the mother. It is not surprising that something so intimate
and human should be the scene of our first trembling experience of
the meaning of trust, a variable that is closely related to our unfolding ability to believe in the world and in others around us.

What begins with another person grows in a social or community setting. That is one of the best arguments for an organized
church; it is meant to be an assemblage of people, a believing community that stands around us at our baptism to affirm us and to
provide the environment of interpersonal support in which our
capacity to believe is differentiated and strengthened.

Perhaps the ancient title Mother Church is not an irrelevant
or merely sentimental statement after all. It catches the essential
responsive quality of the Christian community as the continuing
environment for our development in faith. A church is a nurturing

community concerned with our growing toward a mature position within it. This is a very different feeling from a church that sees baptism as a largely social ceremony and unrelated, in any way that makes a difference, to a growing reality known as faith.

No one, as the tradition of the church attests, expects the infant child to possess fully developed faith. The whole practice of the church has always acknowledged this. Faith needs the context of adult believers in order to grow. When the church senses itself as a living mystery, as a people rather than a bureaucracy, then it becomes an authentic mystical and transforming presence in the world. That is what is meant by a faith community, a gathering of believers who understand faith in terms other than submission; it may not be able to put this into words, and so it intuitively employs the fundamental language of the Spirit, that of myth and symbol.

When faith is merely imposed and can easily be perceived as impersonal and demanding, it is a shell that does not touch or express human experience or longing. Only a living faith can be spoken of in symbols like the kingdom and the treasure. Inconsistent, intermittent, or shallow styles of believing cripple rather than enlarge the growing person's capacity to trust or believe. Inconsistency of response is destructive of the growth of moral character. Inconsistency rather than heresy is the greatest enemy of developing faith. And inconsistency is the terrible contribution of people estranged from or psychologically incapable of contributing to the human foundations of believing.

Believing as conditioned by initial trust is not an invitation to gullibility or to inappropriate innocence. As Erickson and other observers have pointed out, the developing person must learn to mistrust, as well as to trust, other persons and events. This is a subtle but significant aspect of believing that is dependent on our overall personal development. We cannot enter a difficult world without a certain measure of sensitivity to its evils and its deceptions. An undifferentiated naïveté about our world undermines our further growth.

Learning to believe includes being able to tell the difference between something or someone believable and something or someone that is not. This is a healthy response that pays tribute to the depth and complexity of human personality; it introduces us to a world in which evil exists in ourselves and in others. Believers live in that contingent world and cannot survive if they are inappropriately and inexcusably innocent.

Faith, as has been mentioned before, focuses for us some of our most essential life experiences, helping us to grow and to be aware of our growth and whether we are achieving the fullness of our unique human identities or not. These experiences transport us from the shallows of existence into the depths where we begin to comprehend everything that is painfully beautiful and occasionally terrifying about the world and other persons. This is the world in which we believe. It is not a child's garden of verses world, but rather it is a difficult and sometimes hostile place in which we will not survive in very healthy conditions without finely attuned senses of what it means to believe.

Believing is risky not because it invites us into the unknown but because it requires us constantly to confront what we actually do know about the world, as a place where we may be hurt, or misunderstood, or left alone in sickness, or in the grip of some other large or small defeat. Faith leads us deeper into reality; it makes living in the real world possible. Faith untempered by a sense of all, which yawns open like a dragon's savage jaw, the incompleteness of ourselves and of the human condition remains in its infancy.

To return to the relational context of believing, we know that faith incorporates us into the mystery of revelation. Believing and revelation may be considered two sides of the same experience. The impulse to believe, to form constructs about the world and our destiny, prods us to become aware, perhaps in small increments of ourselves. So too, as we make firm our grasp on this revelation of ourselves, we are freer to reveal ourselves to others, to communicate our true personalities to them.

This dynamic process is fired by the faith that opens us to the revelation others make of themselves to us. Believing leads to mutual revelation, and the light of this revelation makes clear the way to a faith more securely anchored in the deep waters of mystery. This is a reciprocal process that marks all our days when we are alive to each other; it also enables us to have some insight into the God who reveals Himself as believable in our language and symbols in this exile from Eden that we call the human condition.

Faith calls forth from us as complete a gift of ourselves as we can offer. Living faith is of the entire person, as has been observed, rather than merely of the intellect or the emotions. It is something that we experience truthfully only when we live in a relatively well-integrated fashion. Faith, as the Gospels tell us, makes us whole, not in some pleasant greeting card sentiment, but because it draws forth the realization of the fullness of ourselves through our true personalities.

This cannot be a half-measure thing or an activity in which we seem to be engaged while we are really thinking of something else. Simply said, we must be all there to each other and to God to be believers. Fidelity is threatened if there is a defect in this total response. Believing collapses when what we believe is really divorced from the way we live.

We stop believing when we hold back friendship or any kindred response that depends on whether our investments of ourselves are genuine or not. Instead of believing, we sometimes only think about believing; we make a check mark on some creed as a security measure, but this restricted view blinds us to full participation in religious reality. We take ourselves out of the environment in which faith lives, missing thereby the authentic religious experiences of our lives.

Faith is, therefore, not merely intellectual, and obedience to authority cannot consist only in accepting certain statements about faith. The obedient element is surely present in believing but, again, this is far more as it is found in friendship and love, the analogies that Jesus himself habitually used to distinguish his kingdom from the authoritarian religious structures of his own day.

The obedience of faith, like that of friends to each other, asks us to listen to and respond to the depths of our honest experiences, to what, when we are open and true, we recognize as taking place in and between ourselves and others. It is obedience to our own truth and our own lives that is the essential psychological note of the true believer.

Faith orients us to greater life, to bringing more of ourselves and of others alive than before we began to believe. Through faith we become more present to ourselves, to our neighbor, and to God. Through faith we continue to grow in these relationships, sensing more deeply as time passes how they encompass and reflect the essential religious themes of the Gospel, meeting and loving, dying and rising, waiting and being filled.

We learn the profound and mystical language of believing, recognizing God's truths for us in the thousand glimpses we get of Him in the activities and aspirations of everyday life. Believing breaks us open to the revelation that energizes the life of the Spirit. The church provides and celebrates the human sharing that is the source of our development until we are strong enough to give of our faith to make others whole.

Chapter Four

Incarnational Faith

We all know the experience of suddenly seeing something with which we are familiar in a new way or in a fresh light. It can be something as simple as the sunrise, an old friend, or some truth about ourselves as when we are surprised by our image in a store window. We say spontaneously that this is like seeing it "for the first time." We have also known those moments of insight when we suddenly identify, through the words or symbols of another, a profound truth of our own experiences.

We say, for example, "That makes sense of the way I have felt." Or, in a slightly different vein, "That's the way I have felt about it for a long while, but I never understood it until now." These human discoveries are only a small portion of the bulky catalogue of surprises that fill a growing life.

Other aspects of ourselves and our world exist and cannot easily be seen in fresh perspectives. We have stabilized convictions or ideas about ourselves and others that we do not really examine because we feel we know just about everything about these subjects. Our religious faith is one of those dimensions of experience we sometimes never hold up to the light for a fresh examination. Yet, whether we notice it or not, faith as a living part of our personalities is constantly changing. We must find the right light of honesty in which to view faith as a growing part of ourselves.

The Second Vatican Council held faith up to the light in an extraordinarily human and sensitive manner. Through their reflections, the bishops of the world made it possible for us to look freshly at something we had considered as resistant to change as the rock of ages. Faith thus became a more exciting and relevant subject as it was perceived in relationship to the great struggles of humankind for individual and social development.

We are familiar with outdated static and a concrete concept of faith, a notion that, as we have noted, is being revived by the so-called Reform of the Reform—a rock as reliable as Peter on which to build our creed. We lose the dynamic meaning of belief if we return to the illusory certainty of religious truths told in concrete language, one of the objectives of the movement to overturn Vatican II.

It remains necessary for us to walk slowly around the vital concept of faith, which remains the energy source for a deep and true understanding of modern theology and pastoral reflection. It is even more important as Pope Benedict XVI's Reform of the Reform seeks to modify the documents of Vatican II and read them by nineteenth-century moonlight, the symbol of time, instead of in the high noon light of the revealing sun that is the symbol of eternity.

Faith was once conceived of as opening us to a world we could not otherwise see; it alerted us to a coexistent spiritual world that hovered somewhere just above this one like a tide of pure white clouds that would one day wash the earth free of its grime. Such faith elevated us and, in a sense, rescued us from all that was purely natural; it enabled us to affirm what was not immediately visible: the realm of spiritual reality that was conceived of as distinct from and superior to the order of our general human experience.

This faith was something for which we could pray, although it was something we could never merit; it demanded surrender of the self, and as a powerful way of structuring our inner and outer worlds, it had enormous practical consequences for the way we conducted our lives. This faith was important because its possession determined our salvation.

The church's concern about this style of faith led it on occasions to be quite insensitive in its dealings with the customs, feelings, and world views of those peoples to whom the Gospel was to be preached by bands of heroic missioners. They were pagans, unbelievers, the spiritually unwashed, who had to be invested at all costs with saving faith.

Some old applications of this medallion-like faith not only turned people away from what was natural, but also devalued the very concept of the natural, perceiving people's inner states as flawed with inadmissible desires and tendencies. These latter included what we now recognize as some of our healthy aspirations, as well as our emotional lives, which, according to this former outlook, had to be tightly supervised and controlled.

Buttressed by the assurances of authority, this style of belief was demanding in one way but a sure thing for salvation in another. Some of the principal stresses of this rather elementary notion of faith—an oversimplified version that prevailed in many ordinary peoples' lives—were those in which faith was tested by a struggle that generally pitted the inner spiritual person against the outer fleshy person.

Just persons, according to the scriptures, lived by faith, but in this version, they did it through maintaining a basically antagonistic relationship with their own personalities. The articles of practical faith that received paramount moral emphasis centered on men's and women's sexual understandings and behaviors. Indeed, in the view of many ecclesiastics, these still constitute the crucial test of the faithful person.

This manner of looking at the world and themselves led people to experience tension between the spirit and the flesh as well as between anything that was proud and stubborn in themselves and everything that was lofty and redemptive in the spiritual sphere. This faith urged them to give up themselves, their ambitions, and the world itself, promoting a functional estrangement from themselves and their possibilities.

Tragically, in the long run, this is what Pope Benedict XVI's Reform of the Reform intends to restore. This is familiar material, of course, but people continue to reflect and talk about it precisely because the imprint of this faith on their own self-awareness has been so profound and, in many cases, so hurting as well. The spite of many rueful Catholic nostalgia books and plays attest to that.

Such faith, thought to be validated by its strictness, possesses a quality of demand but little of celebration. It is not surprising that many people became confused or angered at a faith that imposed a meaning on themselves and their lives that did not seem to match their own experience. That this type of faith supervised from the outside offered meaning and achieved results is undeniable.

We must now investigate what happens to our self-understanding when we get a fresh and unexpected perspective on faith. This new angle of vision on faith may generate that sense of surprise and elation that accompanies our recognition of an understanding that has been forming inside of us for a long time.

If faith is something that can be separated neither from personality nor from life, then the previous tendency to find its tests in the antagonism between the spirit and the flesh, or between the pride of intellect and the grace of obedience, must be reinterpreted. The eyes of faith do not, in fact, focus always on another world that is totally beyond and different from this one in character and expectations. To recognize believing, as much a part of us as our breath or our pulse beat, means that the eyes of faith allow us to see more clearly the never-ending efforts of men and women to understand themselves and their destinies.

Faith that is incarnational enables us to see more and to do it not from a place of exile but from the middle of our earthly journey. This is precisely the shift of viewpoint given to us through the rediscovery of living faith by modern theology and that is in danger of being repudiated again by the Reform of the Reform.

The New Testament message emphasizes that God so loved the world that he sent his only begotten son to it. The Father has chosen to reveal himself not in an invisible way but through a faith made concrete in the humanity of Jesus. Jesus as Lord comes to show us how to live life rather than how to escape life; he spares himself nothing of human experience except sin and, in a way that reveals the mythic language of faith very clearly, speaks in parables and stories through which we can recognize the stories of our own lives.

Jesus asks for belief in himself, a human transaction dependent upon our willingness to grow as fully as possible in our efforts to respond to him. Jesus compares the mystery of his relationship to the church with the human relationship between bride and groom. There is nothing in his preaching or in his life that suggests that the reality of faith precludes the hard but joyful realities of this life, which we share with each other.

Faith that is centered in this life, that understands itself as proclaiming the kingdom that is in our very midst, awakens us to a sense of ourselves as living in and by the Spirit that has been given freely and fully to us. In other words, incarnational faith preached by Jesus enables us to understand our lives and, far from estranging us from our inner states, makes it possible for us to identify the yearnings, conflicts, and other important aspects of our experiences as essentially sacred. Incarnational belief opens us, of course, to a meaning larger than our own small lives, but it does this through helping us look more deeply into, rather than away from, ourselves.

This is the restored sense of faith that emerged from Vatican Council II and is being suppressed by the fearful crusade of Pope Benedict XVI's Reform of the Reform. It is of such faith that the remarkable document on *The Church in the Modern World* speaks its most eloquent phrases. Indeed, it is through its recognition of the intimately human nature of our faith response that the Council proclaims clearly the necessary conditions of freedom and respect that must surround an individual's affirmation of his or her own religious belief.

A description of faith that appeared shortly after Vatican II catches these notes quite well. "Christian faith is a claim to an accurate understanding of this world, human existence and the gracious Being of God; an understanding which is given in the being, life, actions and teachings of Jesus Christ; and one which calls for and makes possible the humanization of men and the worship of God the Father, in a community witnessing to the presence of His Kingdom on earth."

Faith gives us a way of understanding this world in Jesus; incarnational faith awakens us to life in all its dimensions and enables us to see how religious reality is interwoven with our own experiences and cannot be separated from them. Far from being separate and distinct, something to which we can only aspire if we empty ourselves of our human cares and yearning, faith reveals itself as necessarily connected with our personal growth.

The seeds of faith are sown deeply in human personality, and they do not contradict, although they are conditioned by human nature and by the formational psychological experiences through which we achieve our own unique identities.

Such faith is geared not to control but to growth. It lights up the meaning of this world, allowing us to see the pathway we must follow if, individually or collectively, we are to achieve our destinies as God's children. To become fully human becomes the task of the religious person. This is the first response of believing that men and women have possibilities, that our faith must be concerned with these, or we will never discover or understand ourselves.

If faith did not allow us to believe in this world and in each other, then we would all be better off quitting it for the mountains and the monasteries, abandoning it to its misery and final apocalyptic death throes. This has never, however, been the tone or the fundamental intuition of Christianity. The Gospels, and the church's teaching of them, even when it was confused about their literal meaning, has always been concerned with the dignity and worth of every person.

It is difficult to speak about self-fulfillment in an age in which movements aimed at expanding, coddling, or making the self central in everything are so numerous and are frequently characterized by shallowness of both concept and operation. Self-fulfillment has come to sound like some kind of selfish joyride that concerns itself with sensual pleasure more than spiritual reality. But fulfillment is a fair enough name for what Christians seek for themselves and other when they live by faith.

At the heart of it, incarnational faith opens men and women to life and to what it means if we have personal beliefs in Jesus. This necessarily turns us back to experiencing and expressing incarnational faith at the numerous crossroads of choice that intersect the path of our development.

This struggle to respond to our fundamental human challenges involves us in a dying and rising that recur, like the theme of a great symphony, as the resonations of our faith in the life of Jesus. A deep faith opens us to the essential Gospel experience; anyone who tries to love necessarily re-creates and reexperiences the incarnational rhythm of the life of Jesus. Faith recognizes the patters of birth, death, and resurrection that are the determinative experiences through which we know the mystery and meaning of our existence.

Incarnational faith is connected with a progressive and ever-finer self-definition. As has been mentioned before, faith as revelation initiates an awareness of our true selves and the nature of our relationships with each other. Faith is concerned with ourselves and others; its test, far from being limited to certain aspects of our behaviors, such as the sexual, centers on everything about us when we stand face to face, at all the levels of our being, with each other.

Incarnational faith, by its very nature, is never perfectly or fully developed. As we strive to respond, it opens us further, helping us, at levels for which properly descriptive words may not yet be available to us, to grasp some of our own significance and to sense our participation in the *Mysterium Tremendum et Fascinans* of existence as we are in the world as it is.

Through this faith we understand the continuity between our human experiences and our ultimate fulfillment in God. There is nothing that God asks of us that contradicts or destroys anything that is healthy about our humanity. Only such faith can illumine the growth of marriage, the mystery of creativity, or the wonder of our differences from each other.

It is obvious that the faith that successfully interprets and sustains the meaning of human experiences has powerful effects on those who affirm it. This has been true of deeply held beliefs all through the course of history. It also explains our yearning to believe, and sometimes our willingness to believe in outlandish things and individuals when we are denied richer and fuller explanations of our own existence. Belief that matches our urge to grow not only confers a sense of significance on us, but it also gives us a sense of direction. That is why Jesus says, "I am the way."

Faith in him does not move us to look at the human person and see less; it urges us to see more by pressing us to come to terms with everything human about each of us. Faith allows us a better sense of ourselves and moves us toward more honest self-understanding, making us face the evil, as well as the good, that lies within ourselves. Only as we understand the elements of our personality can we forge the identities that best express our human individuality. Believing is very closely tied up with this identification process that never takes place outside of it. Incarnational belief, in other words, does not operate in a vacuum or as though humans and their culture had no effect on the possible development of belief itself.

Anyone who is conversant with the psychological and sociological research on the nature of religious belief will admit that although the measures and modes of its expression are still in need of greater refinement, they catch some of the dynamic of incarnational faith. It has been suggested by Thomas Droege that faith develops in accord with the major growth challenges of the individual man or woman. Only the approach to faith that flows from this central notion of growth offers the possibility of integrating the wide range of human experiences that eventually shape us and our way of believing. These begin, as has been mentioned earlier, with the basic and unconscious experience of trust during the first months of life.

This sharply conditions, for good or for evil, the child's sense of expectation toward the world as a friendly and dependable place. Individuals who do not experience adequate trust at this stage may spend the rest of their lives searching for it and may, in fact, find that it is always difficult for them to profess an act of faith in other persons or institutions. Denied the nurturance of a trustworthy environment, individuals begin life with a major handicap in developing their faith in people or in God.

This is not to say that later relationships cannot help individuals greatly in understanding and experiencing the meaning of faith, although such happy endings cannot be counted on. Children who are not believed in will find it difficult to believe in themselves or in the world in which they must grow and live.

So, too, in the developmental process, children must gradually achieve a sense of autonomy. Without this, individuals cannot come to a sense of their own separateness or define themselves in terms of their own purpose. The struggle for autonomy is the struggle for healthy independence, and this is also strongly conditioned by the human relationships that surround persons in their earliest years.

As Droege observes, "The infant's basic faith in existence, which is the lasting treasure saved from the first developmental stage, must not be jeopardized by the sudden violent wish to have a choice." It is a time of struggle and conflict within as well as outside the individual. This move toward a sense of the self is just as important in moving toward adult faith as it is in the general process of growing up.

Individuals who are not independent, who cannot choose for themselves, have difficulty in sorting out their own experiences of themselves or of others. As individuals move deeper into the world of reality, as they find that they must define their own autonomy in relationship to persons who are separate from them and who possess identities and rights distinct from their own, a major step is made toward the awareness of self that is an integral aspect of deepening their capacities to believe more for themselves than on the words of others as they mature.

The next challenge of faith parallels the tasks of individuals pass-ing through adolescence during which they must come to terms with themselves and with investing themselves in commitments of one kind or another to others. The well-publicized adolescent search for identity finds young persons dealing with the significant factors that they must understand if they are to draw close to others in intimacy. The principal challenge is concerned with the mean-ing of fidelity, with the ability of individuals to give themselves to other people or causes.

Only when they master this can they possess their identities as believable and believing individuals who can move in and through the lives of others under their own psychological powers. There is no way individuals can commit themselves if they lack this sense of who they are and how they differ from others; they simply will have nothing with which to relate to others. This achievement of identity is a necessary foundation for any adult belief or relation-ship to God Himself.

While these reflections on the overall process of human growth are necessarily abbreviated for this discussion, it is still easy to see how these various challenges of development are essential to the full-bodied act of faith we expect to find in adults. This kind of believing does not arrive full blown or independent of the people and processes through which an authentic sense of the self and its capacity for commitment is derived. Faith is the kind of thing we learn as we learn to become ourselves.

Faith runs through the personality as the bloodstream does through the body; it not only gives life to the person, but it is also affected notably by the overall health of the individual. The human person, the perennial believer, simply cannot be divided up accord-ing to the fashion that allowed us once to speak of faith as a re-stricted operation that concerned only the person's intellect or will.

Faith is more pervasive than that and must be considered in relationship to the total presence of an individual in life. To oversimplify for the moment, the less persons grow to their own individualities, the more hampered they will be in developing their religious faith. On the other hand, the more fully human persons become, the more capable they are of exercising vibrant, searching, and satisfying religious faith.

Religion has suffered a twin kind of difficulty for many generations. Viewed by social scientists and medical specialists, as we have observed, it has often seemed a neurotic disorder, the manifestation of the search for magical solutions of life's difficulties, or the gropings of persons who have never satisfactorily resolved their relationships to their parents. That is the kind of religion that can rightly be classed as the opium of the people.

On the other hand, ascetic theologians have been as unkind to religion in quite another way. They heavily mortgaged it, making its highest expressions and experience the property of persons who seemed to disown or detach themselves thoroughly from their own human experience. Mysticism became the function of the well-keened psyche, the final triumph of the person who had vanquished the body in the name of spiritual glory.

Both of these views have made it difficult to look at religious faith as an aspect of the normal healthy personality. The research that has been prompted by the theoretical work of the late Gordon Allport has done much to restore a sense of balance about the place of religion in life. No longer need it be conceived of, in its highest form, as the exclusive property of overspiritualized mystics.

Allport suggested that religious faith could be conceived of on a continuum, the poles of which could be labeled intrinsic and extrinsic. Allport distinguished between these contents by identifying intrinsic religion as a master motive through which individuals can organize and understand all the experiences of their lives. Intrinsic faith, in All-port's view, is a well-developed and mature kind of religious belief.

On the other hand, however, extrinsic religion represents the compartmentalized and quite external form of religious behavior that has no roots in the individual's personality. Far from being that through which persons are able to judge their actions and guide their lives, extrinsic religion is a utilitarian and instrumental phenomenon that individuals use to fulfill obligations, allay fears, and to hold on to for the sake of their own salvations.

This is the religion of immature or underdeveloped persons whose other convictions parallel the shallow quality of their religious orientations. In further research, for example, Allport sought to demonstrate that racial prejudice was frequently found among people who could be described as extrinsically religious; it was not found in subjects judged to possess more mature religious outlooks.

Essentially, extrinsic religion represents a nonintegrated value, the significance of which is grasped only superficially and the effects of which are found minimally in the way people direct their lives. It is closely akin to the religion of childhood, an unquestioned inheritance that is accepted on the authority of those who instruct the individual in its tenets. It never moves much beyond this in the life of the extrinsically religious person.

Maturely religious persons, however, pass through a crisis of belief in which they question what they have received from others in order to test it against what they have learned from their own experiences. Some persons abandon religious convictions of a formal sort at this time of crisis in their lives, sometimes because the fundamentalistic beliefs in which they were reared no longer seem adequate to explain the universe or their knowledge of it. Others turn back from the crisis to hold on to the faith that seems endangered by previously unthinkable questions.

Growing persons, however, accept the challenge of self-examination and transform their faith through a process of internalization at this stage of their lives. Now they believe for themselves rather than on the authority of someone else. The outcome of developed religious faith is quite parallel, in Allport's design, to the self-responsible characteristics of the mature individuals who judge their own experiences in the light of the evidence they are able to procure for themselves.

This conceptualization of religious faith enables us to understand it as a developmental challenge, an invitation to growth. As such, it is no different from any other developmental problem of human beings. They can, after all, be challenged by crises for which they are not prepared; their general developments can be arrested by a complex of social forces and pressures; they can advance into the mature years of life with the psychological equipment of an adolescent.

One must look beneath the appearance in order to discover the true psychological state of the individual within. Religious faith seems to be correlated with the other developmental processes; it does not operate independent of them. Although Allport's schema has been subjected to an array of technical and theoretical criticism, it has proved durable and, in the words of Yale Professor James E. Dittes, it has shown a considerable promise of surviving its obituary.

Most of the research that has employed the intrinsic-extrinsic paradigm has tended to support Allport's general outlook. Indeed, the study of the priests of the United States, conducted through the Psychology Department of Loyola University of Chicago, addressed itself, in part, to the quality of faith of the subjects of the investigation. The results of this study demonstrate the richness of Allport's conceptualization as well as the developmental nature of religious faith.

In conjunction with the other instruments and extensive interviews carried out during the pilot projects and actual study, a special maturity of faith scale was developed that enabled the researchers to make judgments on whether the developmental level of the faith of the respondents reflected their overall personal development. The main body of the research made it possible to assign American priests to various categories reflecting the stage of their psychological development. These were labeled the maldeveloped, the underdeveloped, the developing, and the developed.

In the maldeveloped category were those persons who, although still functioning in the priesthood, gave evidence of serious and chronic psychological problems that interfered in a marked way with their personal and professional lives.

The underdeveloped did not manifest such serious difficulties; rather, they reflected a failure or inability to come to terms with the adult challenges of psychological growth. They were considered underdeveloped in that their psychological ages did not match their chronological ages. Although they looked adult, and had adult responsibilities, these people had generally failed to resolve the tasks a person must face in the adolescent stage of life.

The developing group was comprised of individuals who, although they had been arrested in their growth for a time, had begun to grow again and to deal with the unfinished business of their personal developments. There was a great deal of energy in this group, a clearly dynamic cluster of individuals for whom the pursuit of unfinished growth had become the most important business of their lives.

The developed group of priests represented the individuals who had dealt successfully with the various stages of their lives, had developed their capacities well, and who, although not absolutely perfect, represented what we understand to be psychological health.

In those aspects of the research that investigated religious faith, it is fascinating to observe the gradations of faith that seemed to follow closely on the subjects' levels of personal development. The maldeveloped showed the greatest number of characteristics of extrinsic faith. The underdeveloped, while more advanced than the maldeveloped, still evidenced more signs of extrinsic faith than either the developed or developing groups.

Interestingly enough, the priests in the developing group manifested a slightly higher index of intrinsic religious faith factors than did those in the developed group. The three groupings, however, were more intrinsic in their religious faith, in a statistically significant way, than the maldeveloped group of subjects.

Why did the developing group seem at least equal to the developed group in the nature of their intrinsic religious faith? The answer was probably connected with the fact that they are more vitally involved in dealing with their psychological growth, more excited about it than any of the other groups in the study. While relatively complete integration of personality is obviously a desired stage of development, the rediscovery and pursuit of this seems to activate a person's energies in a quite remarkable way.

This is also evidenced on another psychological test, the Personal Orientation Inventory, on which the developing group scored more highly than any of the other groups. To come psychologically alive is a process that has profound effects on all of a person's behavior. It seems, in other words, that when persons shake off the lethargy of arrested personal development, the intensity of the experience is reflected in some way in everything they do, including the way they score on psychological tests.

They exhibited an exuberance that reflected the dynamic of growth that had been reengaged. It was not surprising to find individuals who could be classified as developing slightly more intrinsic in their orientations than even the developed. They presented themselves with questions for which they previously thought they had the answers and they were, in some sense, enjoying the ambiguity of the experiences. It was still difficult for them to test the nature of their religious faith and to peer into their own psychological adjustments, especially if this has been embarrassingly preadolescent.

There is, it would seem, a remarkable positive trust in human persons through which they move themselves forward when they have at last come in contact with the real heart of their own life experiences. There is an overflow, a sense of feeling alive, that accompanies discovery of new depths both in oneself and in one's faith.

The data of this study support the general concept that the quality of people's religious faith is inseparably related to the levels of their psychological development. Faith does not stand alone or outside the personality; it is something we understand only if we understand the persons who exercise it.

Several questions arose in the light of these findings. First of all, one could lay aside the contention that religious faith is merely a neurotic outcropping. It was clear that the deepest and most functional religious faith was a property of the individuals who had the best sense of themselves, their own powers, and their purposes in life.

People who believed maturely also related to themselves and to their neighbors maturely. They had dealt with the questions of life that mark humans off as separate from the other orders of creation. With authentic awareness, they had learned some of the lessons of loving, the highest expression of which had always been conceded to represent the highest operational definition of religious faith.

This is not to deny that neurotic religion can exist; it manifestly does in the lives of many persons whose needs give shape to the world they inhabit. Their faith generally reflects something about their overall adjustments; as persons are, so they seem to believe. There is nothing startling in this, although it was refreshing to find evidence to support it.

Secondly, mysticism cannot be the exclusive property of people who, in some arduous fashion, overcome the body in order to live almost exclusively the life of the spirit. This is to make the richest expression of religious faith a function of the disintegrated personality. We may have to look much more carefully at our discussions of psychological adjustments, and it is difficult to imagine that psychological adjustments should be absent in the lives of persons who live by a deep and lively faith.

What is truly mystical may, in other words, be present in the intensity of life of persons who are psychologically well adjusted. They are able to love and trust others deeply; they have a sense of possession of themselves and a capacity for entering into life in a profound way. Mysticism may be made up of such experiences rather than of the extraordinary and sometimes seemingly bizarre behaviors with which it has often been described.

Mysticism, in other words, is found in the heart of human experience rather than at its remote and inaccessible edges. Perhaps we have overlooked the healthy kinds of adjustment that seem to be present in the lives of great figures, such as Teresa of Avila, and distorted what seems to be other than this. Many people resist this interpretation of profound religious behavior, finding it too prosaic and too unromantic. Nonetheless, if religious and healthy personal growth go hand in hand, then we must put mysticism back into a more realistic psychological perspective.

Thirdly, it is clear that the unity of human experience is attested to by both Allport's theory and the cited research. Humans cannot be effectively divided into separate spheres, even in the name of religious faith. It is difficult to find a dividing line in the human personality according to which we can set the sacred on one side and the secular on the other. It seems no longer profitable to maintain the old distinctions of mind and body and flesh and spirit, which crystallized the antagonisms that estranged humans for so long from a proper sense of their own unity.

The emerging religious consciousness of our time turns humans back to themselves to the task of feeling again the oneness of the personality given to them by God. One can no longer suppose that religious persons search for a spiritual order that is separate from their human experiences. The unity of life in a totally redeemed universe must be reasserted in order to heal the wounds from which men and women have suffered because of the exaggerated dualism that had disembodied the things of the spirit for such a long time.

Humans cannot be approached only on the spiritual plane. They must be approached as full persons. Religious categories must be capable of being discussed in terms of human experience in order to end the estrangement that history has introduced into the person's sense of his or her own personality.

Fourthly, serious questions with implications for everything from catechetics to the liturgy must be asked in view of the relationship between full personal growth and a well-developed religious faith. The reason is clear: Most people do not possess a fully developed personality and do not have a fully developed religious faith either. Those who are alive psychologically and religiously may be close relatives to the individuals who are categorized as developing in the study of American priests. They are, in a respected ascetical phrase, "in via." They understand that the Christian journey is one of growth toward a goal they have not yet achieved.

The excitement lies in the possibility and promise of the goal, in the conviction that it endures against the ravages of time and space, and in the commitment to the experiences that bring human beings closer to it. Is it impossible, one might ask, for a severely neurotic person to have mature faith? It may well be, but it is not impossible for a neurotic to have a maturing faith.

If the Christian life is a dynamic, process-oriented experience built on the unitary nature of personality, then these ideas need not estrange us from traditional positions. Indeed, one might return to the history of ascetic literature in order to rediscover the images of growth that have always pervaded it. The understanding that the person is made to grow and to fulfill a destiny that is at once religious and personal is hardly a new idea to anyone who has ever read the New Testament.

Chapter Five

Doubting

Faith and doubt have traditionally been contrasted with one another. We are familiar with the hesitations that earned the apostle the title "Doubting Thomas." Then, there is the indictment of certain people because they seem to have "little faith." On the other hand, the proverb tells us belief is strong enough to move mountains. What, in our age of sophisticated inquiry and discovery, can we, in fact, believe at all if we are subject to doubts; or, on the other hand, can we achieve any measure of belief if we never doubt at all?

Doubt has generally been presented as failure, not just of nerve but of the whole believing system, something like a moral fault for which a person must be held accountable. There is, for example, an idea of doubt as a conscious choice not to believe, a deliberate flirtation with the rejection of religious faith. This type of doubt is always considered to be destructive, something dangerous in the air like an infection that eats away at the foundations of religious institutions.

This doubt courts attention, the kind of notoriety through which individuals define themselves against the church of which they have been members or against the faith in which they once believed. Such doubters invite

censure from their religious groups and may even be labeled heretics or apostates, the indications that doubt has metastasized within
them so that their whole belief system has been eaten away. They
test positive for unbelief.

Doubt has also been associated with a kind of weakness that carries the aura and betraying odor of a dissolving moral fiber or a readiness to yield to wavering thoughts about faith. This doubt is judged
a personal rather than a public failure. Nonetheless, those guilty of it
seldom earn the public censure of their religious institutions.

Such people do not seem vitally concerned with official church
affiliation; their lives make little room for formal religion. In the
judgment of self-styled true believers, they seem to have made
friends with the world rather than with God. Such people are
generally prayed for rather than condemned.

Doubt has also been popularly considered as a species of temptation, a presentation in an attractive way of the alternative of non-
belief, the choice of which would constitute a major sin. Here,
again, we have a private rather than a public choice through which
individuals align themselves with the forces opposed to those of
righteousness and fidelity. This temptation is often said to enter a
person's consciousness through the influence of pernicious teachers,
godless scientists, atheistic revolutionaries, or some other easily categorized group whose members seem at odds with the traditional
expressions of faith.

In a familiar scenario of acquired doubt views, it as a temptation that rises like a snake from the basket of college life in which
they are thought to fall in with unbelieving companions, gradually
shedding their faith much to the consternation of their priests and
their families. Such a loss of faith must be admitted and confessed
if such "fallen aways," as they have been called, are to reintegrate
themselves into the group of believers they left behind when they

dropped out of their belief traditions. Only the institution can absolve and readmit them to the church community after such a breach of believing.

Doubt, in any of these guises, has always had a bad name. However, we cannot look at doubt only in an oversimplified and negative fashion. It may be true that ten thousand questions, as Cardinal Newman said, do not constitute a single doubt, but would any good questions ever be asked if we did not question something about our environment at one time or another?

The Christian life is poorly served by those models that portray it as a determined march forward of Christians with jaws set, eyes unblinking, and minds closed against all questions or uneasiness. Such unwavering belief invites us to walk through the valley of death without fear because of our trust in God. Such serenity, however, may come only to those who have, in fact, asked very serious and probing questions about the beliefs that illuminate the mystery of the universe and the suffering in their own lives. It may be inhuman and insensitive not to raise questions or to silence the spirit of wonder about life and its ingrained and transcendent mystery.

A church denies the right of its poets to question the mystery of existence at great dangers to itself. Poetry is, after all, the native language of faith. So the poets who ride before us into the darkness sense and deal with significant human questions far before the rest of us feel their slightest impact on us.

Poets and seers do this not out of intellectual pride or ambition but out of constitutional necessity, because they are attuned to the developing situations that will ultimately touch and affect all of us. Can the language of myth, which has preserved the meanings of faith so powerfully across the centuries, be spoken by individuals who have committed themselves to an excessive literalism about life? Can the poet or the prophet promise not to doubt?

It is difficult to accept or to settle for the dull rhythms that re-assure us when there are times in history when we cannot get by without the unsettling questions of the poets. The poets, whether they are theologians or prelates (and the odds are against this happy combination), cannot perform their function of alerting us to the *Mysterium Tremendum* of our universe unless they are permitted to ask what would seem to be doubting questions.

There is surely some comfort in not doubting, a security akin to that which we think we provide when we buy double locks against the burglars who are often more clever than we are. Our security is spurious and, in the long run, something that plays into the hands of those who would despoil us. Not asking questions has never been a good defense against contemplating the mystery of life.

Another related difficulty is found in the tone of judgmental righteousness that suffuses the condemning pronouncements of self-styled true believers. True believers, or those in charge of orthodoxy throughout history, have always been very hard on their fellow humans. To raise difficult issues seems to fit the curious nature of the human person. A system of belief that has no room for questions leaves very little room for belief or believers either.

It may be a daunting task for many persons even to think about doubt or to inspect at close range some of their inner questionings. There are many reasons for this, including the fact that belief in a strong institutional church may have exercised extensive if very subtle control over their behavior in the formative stages of their lives.

The Catholic Church is a good example of this because, in a fashion that anticipated the work of psychologist B. F. Skinner, many Catholics became self-monitoring. The system of control was so extensive, in other words, that they did not even need supervision in order to maintain themselves within the boundaries of acceptable reflection about their faith.

The guilt attached to doubting—or to other forms of presumably unacceptable thought or fantasy—was sufficient punishment in itself to bring such persons quickly back into the well-marked parameters within which they escaped any feelings of guilt. The reward of avoiding the guilt set off by entertaining novel questions was the major positive reinforcer of orthodoxy, something far more psychological than theological.

This kind of control is extraordinarily advantageous to the institution and, if we focus only on behavior, benefits individuals because it deepens their sense of participation in a meaningful system and inoculates them against the fevers of painful conflicts. It resembles driving within the speed limit out of fear of getting a ticket, a self-monitoring device that is far more effective than external supervision.

Indeed, conflict became a routine psychological experience for those who persisted in questioning systems of discipline or the phrasing of articles of belief that were accepted without question by the churchgoers in the pews around them. Doubter would exile themselves or find themselves exiled.

Because of their inherent need to question, it is not surprising to find that many artists, writers, and poets move outside the institutional church despite their clear connections and fascination with their own Catholic tradition. They feel that their questions take them out of it when, in truth, they are healthy and appropriate expressions of believing.

There is a psychological factor operative in most persons that keeps them from disturbing the waters of their belief systems too much. To question the interpretations of the world that we receive in our childhoods can lead to a dislocation of our entire universe. While many people may be curious, they are not anxious to cause themselves unneeded anxiety or pain by sifting through their beliefs with finely honed inquiries. They do not want to activate any stern test of their beliefs if they can avoid it.

They may not believe everything as it was once told to them, but they are not willing—or perhaps are not able psychologically—to state loudly and clearly that they now question seriously or even reject at least some statements of these beliefs. There seems to be no need for searching questions if the beliefs, in general, seem to serve their religious needs fairly well.

This is not to say that all tests can be avoided; life provides them in illness, tragedies, and a variety of challenging circumstances all the time. These individuals, however, do not wish to be placed in the witness box about their commitment to literal interpretations of belief. They can pass as believers, and, in fact, their true faith may be rather lively. It is simply that the narrow definitions on which they have put such premium, or on the literal concepts of faith they have always accepted, seem like fragile symbols to them, and they do not want to poke into them or dislodge them unnecessarily.

Such persons do not care to become public or even private doubters because the potential pain outweighs the possible discovery that they might thereby make. They would prefer privately to have a sliding scale of investment in the literal claims of institutional religions. They doubt noiselessly so that they disturb neither themselves nor the people in the pews around them.

Doubt remains in the guise of an enemy or at least an unwelcome stranger from whom one is advised to keep at a safe distance. If doubt is an enemy, then it is appropriate to ignore or to crush it immediately. Such have been the tactics employed in the broad treatment of religious doubt through the centuries. Nevertheless, not all doubt is an enemy or even a stranger to human nature or to faith.

As in many other spheres of human activity, doubt may be a positive function of a personality that is engaged in a meaningful way of life. Doubt can be an aspect of healthy curiosity as well as a sign of our seemingly inborn tendency to explore; such responses are very natural and extremely important for us humans.

It is itself doubtful that we could survive very long if we were not capable of questioning the accepted view of things, such as a flat earth, or if we were not open to new signals and new interpretations of reality around us. We would certainly not discover anything or ever create anything new. It would be "Groundhog's Day" for everyone, that is, we would, as in that movie, endlessly repeat the same day forever.

Doubt, pesky and irritating though it sometimes seems, may be an important referent for the developing personality. When we seek a true sense of ourselves, doubt may be best considered, as stated by psychologist Philip M. Helfaer, as an aspect of the ego seeking a full synthesis of itself.

Indeed, modern humans, instead of having their tendency to question suppressed, may need encouragement to ask the right questions and to search courageously for more satisfactory answers. The possibility of doubt as an aspect of healthy self-integration must be viewed again in the perspective of the unbelievable character of biblical literalism and its rejection by a better-educated and more-sophisticated world.

As we stand on the threshold of our new home in the stars, we are, consciously or not, putting aside the representations of the universe that divided it into the antagonistic elements of heaven and earth. Indeed, we find less believable all those interpretations that multiply the subdivisions in our perception of ourselves and the universe around us. When certain statements of faith no longer explain the experience of life satisfactorily, humans cannot keep themselves from doubting.

Doubt can be understood and valued as an integral part of our perennial search—indeed our calling—for more adequate understandings of our existence and experience. This is part of the genius of the religious imagination and the human capacity for discovery, a powerful ally in our efforts to theologize sensitively about life.

Doubt cannot help but come into an individual's life when institutional churches continue to offer interpretations of life that simply do not match the person's own experience or knowledge. This, of course, is the cutting edge of belief itself, the high wire we walk to grow as persons. Individuals who are in touch with their experiences do not readily accept interpretations that contradict those experiences, attempt to suppress them, or to deride their character.

Reactive doubt is inevitable in such situations: "How can I believe what I know cannot be true?" is the question persons ask in this situation. This doubt is not unhealthy because it means an individual is accepting responsibility for what he or she believes in. Individuals do not easily surrender their own convictions when these are not capricious, the fruit of unacknowledged rebellion, or evidence of some other psychological difficulty they do not acknowledge or have yet to resolve.

It is this sense of experience's claims on us—rather than science—that topples the authoritarian insistence on a single view of life. This is not to say, of course, that the human's questioning curiosity inevitably destroys any and every religious belief men and women may have known in their lives. It does, however, challenge the churches to look more deeply into the statement of their beliefs and to examine their imagery and symbolism, so that they may continue to speak the primary truths of faith to everyone in relevant and understandable language.

It is obviously right for churches to speak truly to their people. The issue must, nevertheless, be met head on at that place in life at which we question our inherited belief systems to see if they match our own maturing experiences. After everything is sorted out, after all the reassuring answers have been given, the question becomes for each of us, "What do I really believe in?"

This question disturbs us because it may lead us to reconsider our interpretation of the world and, therefore, to a restructuring of our own lives. The question does not ask what we accept on the word of authority, or what we believe, because to disbelieve would cause pain to those we love; the question directs us to the convictions on the basis of which we lead our lives. It refers us to operational faith, to the principles that guide us in our attitude toward ourselves, our work, and those close to us.

Such a question bids us to inspect our attitudes to see whether they are undergirded by any consistent and embracing philosophy or theology of the world. Honest persons begin by discovering the things in which they truly believe; these may be quite different from the things in which they profess to believe on a more surface level.

In response to this kind of inquiry, some would provide the answer that we must believe in the creed of the church. In fact, this is the very strategy that has been used by churchmen for years and is being employed again by Pope Benedict XVI in his efforts to "reform the reform" of Vatican II.

This emphasis on objective belief tends to separate it from the life experience of the believer; this re-creates, in other words, the old mistake of thinking that the so-called religious element of personality can be abstracted from our motivational system, and that thus excised, it will respond better to creeds enforced with purposeful discipline.

This is an institutional response to anxiety, to the kind of worry that creeps into the souls of men and women when their belief systems are under strain. A difficult state of affairs, no doubt, but it is surely not an abnormal one; nor should it immediately be condemned under the old rubric that doubt and questioning are intrinsically evil. It is not really to deepen faith but to allay anxiety that ecclesiastics speak of an "irreducible minimum" in which a person must believe in order to be counted as a member of the Roman Catholic Church. This underscores the objective literal nature of belief in a manner that destroys the rhythmic interaction between believer and belief that is essential to a personal religious response.

The advantages of an irreducible minimum, or, for Benedict XVI, of the Catechism of the Catholic Church, are very great. This reassures the institution that it knows what it is about, that it is in continuity with its tradition, and that it has not been guilty of misinforming or misleading its believers. It also reassures the institution in terms of its authority and continues a flexing of its orthodox muscles as it reaches out to keep its own believers in a properly responsive stance to its pronouncements.

The latter approach is enormously helpful to some individuals who are in crisis about what they believe in. If the church is there, rising above the postindustrial world as a serene and reassuring presence, then their doubts, or even their need to inspect them, may safely be put aside. These believers find comfort in believing that things do not change in a changing world.

In many ways, this emphasis on certain articles of faith leads to an exaggerated and distorted ordering of beliefs, an outcome of an unconscious need for discipline and institutional order rather than orthodox purity. Such, for example, is the Roman Catholic Church's continued insistence on the discipline of celibacy for its priests.

On the practical level, celibacy for priests is one of the few things in which a person must believe or accept as a demand of institutional faith at the present time. Although this is an extremely strange state of affairs, and is a discipline rather than a dogma, celibacy remains an issue that ecclesiastics do not wish to examine too deeply. Neither do they wish to examine the complexities of celibacy too deeply. Leave it on the surface, caged in, no visitors welcome, and accept without questioning that this is the right thing to do.

Nor do church leaders wish to examine too carefully the theology of the church, the priesthood, or the episcopacy because, at some level of their awareness, they know that such a reexamination may challenge the beliefs they now hold on these matters. While there is wide-ranging theological speculation on many matters within the Catholic Church, presently celibacy is in tight focus because it is one of the few areas in which the authorities of the church can effectively assert themselves.

This reveals how churchpeople can make themselves unbelievable when they do not keep up with their theological, scriptural, or historical studies. They can only defend a tradition built on previous and less-sensitive theological and scriptural foundations. When unexamined and enforced celibacy attains such a centrality, the meaning of faith as a total personal response to life is markedly diminished.

Another difficulty connected with the insistence on an irreducible minimum is that it places enormous burdens on individuals. Must they, in the face of their conscience and careful reflection, force their experiences into a scheme of religious interpretation that simply does not explain them anymore? Is it really the burden of individuals to go on accepting, even at the price of personal conflicts, statements in which they can no longer believe?

The burden, I suggest, is rather on the churches who commit their theologians not merely to restate old beliefs but to help all people to recognize the constantly renewing face of perennial belief. The individual is indeed in a difficult situation when he or she hears, from very high sources in the church, statements that reflect

a somewhat primitive, externalized, and immature concept of the
world of human experience.

It does not help, for example, to have the pope speaking about
the reality of an individual devil in an age in which it is urgently
important for people to come to terms with the evil of which they
themselves are capable. To underscore a devil outside of us is to locate evil outside of ourselves and to excuse us from the penetrating
self-confrontation that is essential to a growing faith. A reassertion
of a literal devil is a throwback that makes it harder rather than
easier to understand the problem of evil.

Helfaer distinguishes two approaches to religious doubt, building on the contrast found between the outlooks of Karl Barth and
Paul Tillich. For Barth, a more fundamentalistic theologian, doubt
was a betrayal. Of it, he says that "no one should flirt with his
unbelief or with his doubt—theologians should only be sincerely
ashamed of it."

On the other hand, Tillich says that "if doubt appears, it should
not be considered as the negation of faith, but as an intrinsic element which was always and will always be present in the active
faith." Helfaer, in his brilliant analysis of religious doubt, contrasts
two psychological types who are characteristic, in the practical
order, of the differing viewpoints of these two great Protestant
theologians.

The conservative position in theology, he suggests, is ordered
to the reduction of the ambiguity found in the symbols of the
religious belief system. The doctrines of the belief system are then
applied as absolutes to the personality. The liberal position, however,
permits far more individual interpretation of the symbols of faith,
especially as they relate to a person's own experience. "In conservative theologizing," Helfaer notes, "the doctrines are applied to the
person, and if he has experiences which do not fit the doctrines, he

is wrong. In the liberal position the individual's experience is more a key to interpreting the religious symbols."

He believes that these approaches, which find their origins in the psychological history of the individuals in whom they are expressed, correspond roughly to the processes of internalization and externalization that have already been applied to the analysis of religious faith. These follow, not in some judgmental sense about the value of one position over the other, but as a consequence of the life history of individuals and in their particular efforts to understand who they are and to define themselves in place and time in a meaningful way.

Helfaer is careful not to pass judgment, as though he were denigrating the conservative position to exalt the liberal view of developmental faith. In fact, he takes pains to avoid this. It is obvious, however, that he finds an acceptable and positive place for doubt in the development of a faith system and that he sees the task of the maturing individual as tied up with a steady self-examination of his own belief.

It is difficult to see how the human person can achieve a higher synthesis of the self if not permitted to question or reassess his or her motives or understanding of life. Mature believers need to doubt in order to get in better touch with themselves and to make their believing more responsive to the reality of their lives and to that of the world around them. This kind of doubt, found in striving persons everywhere, seems to be an aspect of our search for wholeness.

Doubt is, therefore, not merely a careless attitude toward religion or its symbols. It is a painful and difficult process, involving self-confrontation and requiring a serious commitment of the person to the process. It also needs an environment in which it can be carried out without excessive threat being present. In other words, believers must be helped to believe enough in their own searchings so that they can follow them through with honesty and thoroughness. A church must provide these conditions or fail in its mission to preach a faith worthy of humans.

Growing believers need a church that is sensitive enough to their needs and rich enough in its symbols to allow this search to proceed, even on an individual basis, without too much repression out of fear that its own institutional integrity may thereby be damaged. The churches, in other words, need a more profound faith in their people. The question is not whether humans believe in the churches but whether the churches believe in them. The question is not whether the church has a future but whether it believes that the human person has a future.

Any church that represses its capacity to question also cripples its capacity to learn; it may, in the process, severely damage its claims to teach. The issue is one of believability. A church reveals itself as something we can believe in when it permits humans to be themselves and to search, following the rigorous conditions needed to do this with integrity, for the beliefs that will make the seemingly contrary world "transparent to transcendence."

This may require the churches to confront themselves to see whether their priorities make room for men and women who must doubt if they are going to grow. If, on the other hand, the church is more concerned about its own survival than about the growth of the person, it can only restrict the possibilities of the human investigation of existence. Actually, it can only try to retard a journey that persons must set out upon if they are to be believers with any depth at all.

"Blessed are they who have not seen but have believed," is the phrase that has been used against unbelievers for years. It may well be turned against the churches that, in their anxiety to repress doubt, have failed to believe in anything but the most literal interpretation of religious faith.

This foreshortened vision speaks of an institution that does not believe enough in the things that it cannot see, that may have the eyes of faith but keeps them tightly closed. The person's profound need to believe includes the need to doubt and to inquire. Only a church that sincerely believes in men and women as they are and that understands and accepts the rich texture of faith can help human being to become true believers. The faith that makes us whole makes room for questions and for the blessings of endless discovery and surprise.

Chapter Six

The Faces of Fidelity

To the fabled visitor from another planet, fidelity might seem to be something that everybody talks about but nobody does much about anymore. Although fidelity is still an ideal, it does not seem to be an absolute requirement in a supersophisticated world. Fidelity bears the weight of cobwebbed connotations and strikes many as a quaint notion out of the past when people settled for stable, if sometimes romantically undernourished, relationships.

Now, however, men and women question lifelong fidelity as though it were a dream of a madman who only confused human affairs by introducing the idea in the first place. Fidelity, which involves a great deal of believing, has been pronounced, or at the very least, is not defined, in terms of a limited span of time.

The question of fidelity is relevant not only to human relationships, but also to religious symbolism and the institutional churches. If men and women are suddenly proclaiming a new freedom from the iron grasp of an old concept of fidelity, they are also questioning ancient formulas of faith and actively turning away from a whole inventory of respected and presumably stable religious traditions.

It is not just the faithfulness of lovers for each other that is under question at this time; it is also our human capacity to believe in God or in his spokesman for any sustained amount of time. Our present conflicts about fidelity affect people's willingness to enter into institutions that expect them to remain in relationship with them for life. A pervasive contemporary problem, fidelity is one of the dimensions of believing that is most important to understand.

The present questioning, of course, does not reflect so much a desire for limited periods of fidelity in marriage as much as it reveals deep yearning for an unquestioned and permanent fidelity that would be immune to the fierce weathering it experiences in the human condition. Invulnerable fidelity is one person's want, and not getting it, he or she may give up on fidelity altogether. The virtues of infidelity are discussed because this seems to free persons from the situations and relationships that have not worked out or have gone stale, and in which fidelity is a sterile demand for conformity rather than incorporation, through reciprocal believing, into a larger and deeper life.

The desire for such freedom is a search for something other than the human condition, for a time and place where love won't hurt anymore and where we won't have to recommit ourselves every day to the contingencies of life. In a sense, this longing for a more effortless form of believing—fidelity that takes care of itself—is understandable. The strategy of achieving it by undercutting the very notion of fidelity, however, seems strange indeed.

It is also true that although we might like the freedom to be less obsessively faithful ourselves, we are not quite so ready to permit others to be unfaithful to us. Whether this is compounded of self-pity or accurate self-perception is hard to tell; the fact remains, however, that we are far more tolerant of our own ambivalence toward fidelity than we are of the infidelities of others toward us.

There is a large measure of subjective dishonesty symbolized in questioning even the possibility of lifelong fidelity to any promises, whether to marriage, to a belief, or to a vocation in life. Some modern persons are obviously uneasy about their own identities; the cracks in the foundation of fidelity come from the pressures exerted by their own inner problems.

Perhaps we should not be surprised that a generation of Americans plagued with self-doubt and identity crises have special problems with the notion of fidelity. Fidelity, the capacity to dedicate oneself to another person or to a cause, has been described as one of the principal challenges of adolescence, something one must achieve as a prerequisite for reasonable healthy and productive participation in the adult world. Our estrangement from fidelity may be a sign that we have not completed our adolescent growth. The statistics on affairs or about the older marriages that have become dehydrated and are blowing away across the continent may tell us that we have fallen short in our ability to believe in ourselves and in others, and that we are estranged from the meaning of fidelity, rather than that we have outgrown it.

There is also widespread concern that if the present publicized disenchantment with lifelong fidelity continues, society itself will come down in a thunderous and final collapse. In these discussions, the young are the ones usually accused of shaking the beliefs of yesterday by rejecting the institutions of today. Young couples, for example, question the idea of entering into marriage until they are sure they wish to remain with each other; so too, they doubt the value of attending church to pay tribute to a belief about which they have little conviction.

These reactions seem alarming to an older generation that never felt it could afford even the luxury of asking such questions. Older people, including many churchpeople and good parents, sometimes

seem willing to settle for the appearance of fidelity both in marriage and in church attendance in order to spread some cohesive
paste across the shattered institutions of society. They seem to believe that a little hypocrisy in the service of stability may not be
such a bad thing after all.

Young people may, however, be stalking the concept of fidelity,
looking for the secret that makes things last, as earnestly as anyone
else in society. Although they seem at odds with the generation
that raised them, their yearning for stable and emotionally satisfying relationships are not unlike those of their parents. Some of the
conflict comes from the fact that this issue is so sensitive, springing
as it does from the tender depths in the heart, that people defend
themselves even as they try to speak about it.

The succeeding generations share a sensitivity to and a fear
of the potential for hurt involved in the real-life working out of
fidelity. The young express a somewhat intuitive hesitation about
committing themselves permanently before they are emotionally
prepared to do so. They also seem to mean it when they speak
of wanting relationships marked by the strength of reciprocal
caring.

Members of the older generation, on the other hand, are reap-
ing the fruits of having entered many marriage relationships before they were ready for them and before they even understood
the kind of strength they would need in order to work them
through successfully. Some of these older people are only now
seeking the kind of relationships marked by a deep and mutual
caring, the kind that makes intimacy safe, the very thing they may
have missed earlier.

We may have reached the age in which we can finally get beneath the surface of fidelity, in which we can learn something
richer and deeper and in better perspective than we have been able

to do before. We may not have reached the final season of faithfulness, its farewell performance in the human condition, as much as a chance to look at it closely again.

What may have been taken for granted too quickly about a fidelity that could never be questioned is now being examined by those who want to get at its core value, if they can find it. Men and women want to unearth the roots of fidelity rather than merely be dazzled by its seasonal blooms.

This is not the popular way of looking at our present conflicts over fidelity. Both marriage and the churches are falling apart, according to some commentators; is this true when we look at it more closely? Or are these institutions under stress precisely because men and women seek an experience of faithfulness that celebrates rather than paralyzes their relationships with each other?

It seems unlikely that human beings are giving up on fidelity any more than they are giving up on believing in general. They are rather hoping that they can find a new—and in some cases an easier—brand of fidelity that will serve them, like the psalmist's shield, against all that life can do to vulnerable persons.

In order to understand fidelity or to come closer to a realization of what it demands of us, we must have some understanding of the nature of choice and the demands of freely committing ourselves to other persons or to causes. What is needed is an awareness of the motivations that drive us in certain directions even when we are not completely conscious of them.

Unless we have some appreciation of these, of course, we can never expand our freedom of choice or really commit ourselves to anyone or anything. To become individuals requires a steady increase in our own sensitivity to ourselves so that we can consciously bring into better balance our expectations of fidelity from others and our willingness to respond faithfully to them.

Nor can we be strangers to our own possibilities for deceit, both of ourselves and of others, in the pursuit of temporary and not very satisfying intermediate goals in life. One of the great psychological mysteries of all time centers on the way we can, in fact, choose small rewards, even though we know we are going to pay very heavily for them later on. People have an elaborate catalogue of defenses, not the least of which is the polished rationalization that makes everything, howsoever inconsistent, seem reasonable if not thoughtful.

It is hard to stand at enough distance from ourselves to get this tendency into perspective and, of course, it is still easy to fool ourselves. We must not be naïve about the way we can twist the pattern of our own existence or deliberately misread it in an effort to make the face of reality more comforting to us. We really never get too old to deceive ourselves, and the individual who would master the meaning of fidelity should never lose sight of this.

An appreciation of fidelity also requires an appreciation of the nature of commitment; a commitment can never be effectively defined as something that is done once and forever in life, a point of choice in time when we made some pledge or promise. Commitments are better understood as continuing acts of believing.

The commitment of ourselves to others or to institutions requires a full-dimensioned belief through which we work out our relationships to each other or to these causes afresh every day. As far as commitments go, life begins at dawn for each one of us. We may surround an initial commitment with a ritual and memorialize it in a similar fashion on succeeding anniversaries. These activities, however, are undertaken only to sharpen our focus on the everyday essence of commitment. It is a continuous phenomenon, the meaning of which emerges in the lives of those who know that we do not live on promises made a long time ago but on vows that are deepened with each new day.

The nature of the commitment that enlivens fidelity is not that of some abstract law or prescription handed down by God in the early hours of the human race's existence. Commitment suffers from the clustering burdens of historical settings and examples. Essentially, commitment is centered in a living and developing personal belief in another person.

Commitment is not found in any other form, even though it may be formalized by an institution, such as a church, or spoken of in relationship to the traditions of a race or a family. Commitments are intrinsically personal, always bringing us face to face with other individuals and summoning from us the level of response needed in this situation.

Committing ourselves to each other is always filled with hazards and difficulties because we change so through time; we grow wiser, get sick, change jobs, and move to different localities; we get a new look at things, including ourselves, and we cannot avoid becoming different and, to a certain extent, even estranged from the self we knew at an earlier time. On this strange moving edge of life, we meet and commit ourselves to each other.

Such commitments have meaning when we appreciate and make room for the changes that will necessarily occur in ourselves and in those around us. Sometimes surprising and sometimes expected, they are predictably constant. Fundamentally, our commitments are to growth, to becoming more of ourselves and with an increasing sensitivity to each other. Commitments live in a human setting; that is why they tap into our personal capacities to believe. We live out our commitments through operational belief in each other.

The believing that goes with living fidelity builds on our changeableness in a positive and constructive way. Fidelity that depends on deadened adjustment resembles an uneasy peace in

Northern Ireland or in the Middle East. Anything can disrupt it at any moment. That is why people sometimes feel trapped by fidelity; it seems like a suffocating cloak rather than an aspect of their experiences through which they freely express and expand themselves.

To respond with faithfulness means to continue to change in accord with the changes in oneself and in one's loved ones. None of this is accomplished without sensitivity, communication, and the willingness to make sacrifices in order to share what truly happens in and through one's life experiences.

This is the kind of fidelity in which people grow together; it does not freeze them in space and time but makes room for them to become more mature, to experience unpredictable difficulties and unexpected problems, to grow occasionally at differing rates so that their need to respond to each other becomes more urgent and, in the long run, more fruitful. This fidelity depends on an understanding of one of believing's essential characteristics: its capacity to grow to match the needs and transformations of personality.

Belief is centered not on what we were when we first met, or what we were on our wedding day, our time of ordination or religious profession, or some other occasion on which we crystallized in a single moment our commitments. Fundamentally, our beliefs are in what we can become together, through our reciprocal commitments to growth under the influence of the Spirit.

Our commitments, in the long run, are to this reality, one that never takes care of itself. Belief, contrary to some understandings of it, is not something that, once secured, takes care of us. It is something we work on all the time, a mystery that demands a constant incorporation of the truth of ourselves into the heart of our relationships of fidelity.

Fidelity is not, then, just a stern command never to change but rather a very complicated invitation to continue to grow at the price of changing to some extent each day. This is the way fidelity is kept fresh, the way human beings are able to stay alive and to grow together through a lifetime.

It may be easy enough to apply this to the relationship of friendship or to a marriage, but it is also important to consider this in relationship to institutions like the church. The administrators of these institutions refer to their communicants as "the faithful." They tend to demand certain regular responses that demonstrate the fidelity these people have toward the church's teachings and its moral and dogmatic guidelines and instructions.

The dynamics of fidelity obtain in the relationship between an individual and his or her church in much the way they do between an individual and the one he or she loves. Fidelity is reciprocal wherever it is found, and as the burden can be placed fairly on neither the husband nor the wife alone, so the burden for fidelity cannot safely be placed fully on the faithful.

The other side of the issue asks the churches to be faithful, not just to their historical past or to their traditions, but to the living experiences of growing more deeply in their commitments of service and love to their people. The church's commitment is worked out every day, more personally than officially, when it is pastorally alive to today's men and women.

The essential church is, of course, alive whenever human beings themselves are alive to each other. The administrative church, however, needs to look more deeply at its own commitment of fidelity and at the way it responds to its people. The church can fail in faith, in other words, through an inherent slowness or a reluctance to keep faith with the overall growth of its people.

The feeling of estrangement that fills the corridors of many institutional churches springs from the difficulties these churches habitually court by trying to define too rigidly the nature of their relationships to their people. These churches become estranged because they either never knew or else they have forgotten that their commitments are not to the changeless requirements of membership lists but to growing persons in whom the essence of belief truly lives.

What kills the kind of fidelity that should be found in churches is the previously mentioned confusion of the notions of loyalty and fidelity. Perhaps unknowingly, that is what Pope Benedict XVI has put at risk in trying to return the church to another age. Blind obedience is just not the same as active and searching believing. Fidelity makes room for the latter but not for the former. Loyalty of this kind kills faith and fidelity. Fidelity belongs to the living, to those who still love enough to respond to the impulses of growth even when these demand a constant self-transformation. Pope Benedict seems not to understand that a church is faithful not by refusing to change but by being willing to grow.

The problems of fidelity for institutions are as difficult as they are for individuals. Essentially, however, they are the same. That means that they are intrinsically personal, that they are rooted in the process of continuing growth and developing consciousness that marks the passage of people through life and history.

The churches cannot be faithful unless they are ready always to speak in new languages in order to respond with a full and living faith to the believers they serve. To fail to hear contemporary persons' cries for a richer and deeper grasp of what it means to be faithful and to believe is to misunderstand, misdefine, and ultimately to miss altogether the challenge of fidelity in modern life.

Chapter Seven

Faith and Life

If believing is a central and integrating human response—one through which we know ourselves and our world—what is it that people believe about? In interviews with many people it became clear that the hunger for belief is pervasive and intense, if sometimes unrecognized for what it is. Most people do not identify their own personal searchings for the right kind of lives as explicitly religious activities, and not often as an aspect of theological faith. They are, even the most sophisticated among them, somewhat unselfconscious in their operational everyday believing.

Believing is important to them as individuals, and they also understand that no society can rise or stand for long without it, but active human believing seems to them of a different order from belief in God and supernatural truths. Human believing helps you make it through the night, or at least the darker hours of life, but it is often perceived as something that exists in and between persons and is distinct from the kind of religious faith that is described in catechisms and lettered into creeds. People live by what they style a secular faith, but they are saved by a different kind of Faith—a capital letter phenomenon whose source is in God.

Although there are some theologians and other persons of common sense who have come to identify these experiences of faith as different dimensions of the same thing, the boundary line between them remains fairly rigid and fixed in our common way of speaking and teaching. This is part of the heritage of a divided model of people and the universe as well as a failure to understand that we have only our own languages and experiences with which to speak about our relationships to each other and to God. Rather than raise an argument about why this is so, let us face the fact that we are still far from preaching clearly or in a popular way about the possible coextensive reality of faith in people and faith in God. Perhaps in the everyday lives of those to whom our preachings are addressed, sufficient understanding of this already exists, even though it has not yet been formulated into words.

When we look at believing persons, at those people who identify themselves clearly as religious believers, many of them already have an unnamed sense about the real depth of their human expressions and exchanges of faith. They recite the creed, of course, and were they asked about the content of their faith, they would point to the teachings of their church. Despite that, ordinary persons do not determine their lives on the basis of such doctrines as the Trinity. They are affected by creedal statements, especially insofar as these illumine their sense of values, but the countdown to their most important yeas and nays is marked off on the edges of human experience, on what they have learned to believe about each other in the course of their growth through time.

When we speak about the *sensus fidelium*, the sense of the faithful, we may be referring to this powerful intuition about the rightness or wrongness of certain behaviors or activities that seems to flow out of the bones of the believing community. These judgments, to which we so often turn when theological reasoning fails, are total human responses, the feelings of the group that flow from faith that has become a rich alloy of human experience. When the Christian community, after proper reflection, speaks on some issue, it does not do it in syllogisms.

The reaction is closer to poetry than logic because it represents people drawing on resources deep within them and their life histories. The teachings of faith and human experience that are faithful to their own truths do not contradict each other. Average persons react on the level of what strikes them as right or wrong, quite unconscious of the way faith and experience have been forged into one thing through this judgment. Faith speaks comfortably in a human voice, in tones that reflect a tested capacity to trust mature human reactions to life.

The Gift of Reception

The sense of the community of believers can be roughly defined as that which the larger and healthier portion of believers (*Sanior et Major Pars Fidelium*) accept as believable. This is not an intellectual exercise but a judgment arising from their total personalities, from testing a teaching against their own experiences.

This capacity for discernment by believers has always been respected by the church; indeed, it is referred to as one of *the munera,* or gifts, of the church. Simply stated, no teaching can be proclaimed as true unless it is received, that is, endorsed or accepted as believable by the majority of sound believers. The canon of the books of scripture was determined by applying the test of reception to these varied books.

Examples are found in every century of church history. Even Blessed Pope John XXIII found that one of his encyclicals—that which just before Vatican II directed that Latin be restored as the teaching language in all seminaries—was not received by the faithful and became, so to speak, a Flying Dutchman, lost at sea because it was denied entry at the port of belief. More recently, in 1993, Pope John Paul II tried unsuccessfully to settle the question of whether women could be ordained priests by claiming, in an apostolic letter, that the church lacked the authority to ordain women. He even asked then prefect of the Congregation of the Doctrine of the Faith, Cardinal Joseph Ratzinger, to support it as an infallible document. All of this was, however, to no avail because this teaching has never been fully accepted, largely because the arguments do not correspond with the experiences of the majority of good Catholics.

Perhaps the most famous case of nonreception was Pope Paul VI's encyclical *Humane Vitae*, in which he reiterated the church's traditional rejection of birth control. Indeed, the encyclical caused international upheaval, the assertion of the rights of conscience and, ultimately, the rejection of Paul's teaching. So stricken was he by the failure of this encyclical to be received by the faithful that he did not write another one in the ten remaining years of his papacy.

Faith: Does It Answer or Ask Questions?

Some people build a lifestyle on dogmatic absolutes, threading their way through the human condition by weighing the eternal consequences of each action or decision along the way. The dogmas of heaven or hell are very real to these people as sources of motivation for everything they do from loving their neighbors to keeping the sabbath. Such persons may go through life hearing the music of heavenly choirs or the crackling of flames, but they are not like most ordinary persons who struggle along with not much more than crowd noises in the background. Individuals who regard everything in view of its eternal merits or demerits may obscure their views of life to such an extent that they never do quite understand what it is all about.

Looking at life in terms of its extrinsic rewards multiplies the difficulties in appreciating its intrinsic meaning. It is no secret that fundamentalist faith harbors a traditional distrust and dislike for a great many ordinary life experiences that are counted by most other common people as playful and profoundly human. Such, for example, are courtship, eating and drinking, the use of leisure, and other similar experiences. For most of us, these are judged in the context of our overall lives, in terms of what we mean rather than in terms of what these things, independent of our responses, might mean in themselves. To live a life based on selected elements of a creed closes people to great portions of their experiences and, therefore, to primary sources of faith.

To approach living faith on the level of what goes on and why it goes on in people's lives may seem theologically naïve. We may, however, understand beliefs better in terms of our well-grounded questions than in terms of somebody else's cut and dried answers. A reciprocal relationship exists between human experience and its reflection in a theological view of life, a continuing dialogue between what persons know together and what the poetic language of faith attempts to identify and to put into perspective for them.

This living process allows for growth both in our capacities to believe and in our capacities to translate our experiences into the language of faith. Deep human longings, the unwitting part of ourselves, blend with our capacities to react with wonder to incorporate us into a life where believing is a dynamic human response that opens us to all of God's reality by awakening us to the reality we share with our neighbors.

Human Questions/The Right Questions

What are the basic questions that everyday believers raise and, by so doing, involve themselves necessarily with God? These are the recurrent human inquiries that concern men and women everywhere. It is to these questions that any religious faith or philosophy of life must give some spiritual response if not a detailed explanation. Perhaps the best test of any belief system lies in whether it addresses itself to these questions and with what sensitivity it throws light on the human experience that prompts them in the first place. Faith opens us to and grounds us in the mystery of being alive; it does not make things more mysterious. It makes it possible for us to live in and with our experiences more honestly. It does this in effective language and symbol, or it is talking to somebody other than the human person.

The important questions in life hold no surprises for any of us, unless we have come late to be concerned about or to understand them. Life is not a child's garden of verses, and a sweet and over-simplified faith, much as we might long for it, does an eventual disservice to us as well as to the capacity of religious faith to enter the mystery of existence that includes an often seemingly cruel and contradictory world.

Religious faith is made for tough, human questions rather than for those that are as fragile and sugary as baker's cookies. In proposing the following themes from common questions, I am raising the issues that men and women want to know about, that they want and need to penetrate more spiritually in order to live more purposefully. Humans need to, and do, believe in something, from the Ten Commandments to tarot cards, to address these satisfactorily; they also need the explanatory and supportive help of a sensitive religious belief system in order to speak the credo that provides verbal symbols for the faith that undergirds their lives.

What is existence all about? That is a question that floats near the surface of humanity's consciousness almost all of the time. It is repeated in poems and popular songs as well as in the penny catechism. This subject is debated intellectually, but it rises from deep within the person, and abstract and philosophical responses are seldom adequate. Average persons are not sustained very much by the notion that life is accidental or ultimately meaningless. They experience an inner urge to enter the mystery of their experiences even if they cannot fully explain it, to make their way through the debris of history, and to glimpse some vision that holds it all together and provides some explanation for the juxtaposed cruelties and joys of being alive. People need to believe something about what they know and feel together that acknowledges the difficulty of getting the pieces of life to fit even approximately into place.

A Sense of Being Alive

Hard religious questions have echoed in human consciousness all through history. When the grand design is beyond us, we dig for significance within the restrictions of our own lives and callings. Despite the changes over the centuries, one must wonder whether the person with the routine job who makes his way to and from his Bronx, New York, apartment every day has a clearer view of ultimate meanings than the factory worker in Dickens' London or the farmer battling the seasons on the western frontier. We do not want to believe that we are insignificant, grains of sand lost in the wind-shaped dunes. Men and women have always ached for a sense of something that supports the significance and dignity of their generally anonymous lives. More often than anywhere else, they uncover it in the midst of their relationships with each other.

Meaning in general can only dawn for the individuals who experience specific meaning with another person; the very notion of meaning is otherwise only an abstraction. It is in each other's company that common believers begin the search for a grasp of the difficult questions of why they are alive; it is from the qualities that inhere in what they experience together that they sense throughout themselves the meaning of believing.

Just as an infant's introduction to life depends on his or her first experiences of trust, so our further entrance into practical believing rests on an ever-maturing experience of what it means to be believed in by somebody else and what it means to believe in them in return. Humans can believe in their larger meaning—and in an evolving destiny that makes sense out of all creation—only when they have tasted the experience of believing in relationship to another human being.

The latter is the fundamental transaction that God does not bypass in giving us the gift of faith. We are prepared to understand the world and a faithful God as its creator if we stand on the foundations of a deep life with others. The kind of believing we do in each other is the beginning of the believing we experience in God; God is believable to those who have known believable persons.

Can We Trust God
if We Don't Trust Each Other?

We give each other hints and intuitions of the depths of God's concern and faithfulness through our faithfulness to each other. The believing response, which in itself integrates our world of meaning, cannot be divided up; it is one thing, and the more fully it is experienced with our fellow humans, the more clearly it shades into a deeper sense of God's goodness and presence. How, we might ask, could we ever believe in a passionate God who wants to share His life with us unless we had met someone with whom we passionately wanted to share our own lives?

These understandings are mere hints rather than full explanations, more like a sudden train window view of the Alps in a fog break than a close-up climb of their snowbound slopes, are never yielded once and for all, no matter how eager we may be or even how profound are our communions with other persons. Spiritual insight does not come in chunks but in an emerging pattern that matches and enlarges our own experiences. Our experiences of believing give us a sense of direction and a center of gravity that allow us to pursue the pattern more deeply.

Scenes shift, of course, especially our ever-enlarging and deepening human experiences. Human beings grow and find that their perspectives necessarily change as they develop. We gain new awarenesses and become aware of previously uncharted weaknesses along with the discovery of unsuspected sources of strength. Only believers who understand that active faith is a truly dynamic process rather than a stamped passport can grow old with some sense that they have journeyed through the *Mysterium Tremendum et Fascinans* of existence, that they did not have the curtain down as their train passed through the mountain ranges of wonder, that they did not miss their existence.

We change our notions about this mystery of faith as we pass through various life stages, and we can only do this successfully if, in a very real sense, we keep faith with our transforming selves. We are called on not only to believe in our possibilities, but also to respond to our actualities, that is, to keep bringing forth what is true of ourselves in the face of a wide variety of challenges and difficulties. Faithfulness to the truth of one's person—which, of course, involves us in fidelity to those around us—means that we refine an essential sense of ourselves that remains constant and deepens as time passes.

That reliable core is what we recognize as trustworthy in each other; it also enables us to believe in an essentially responsive and faithful God. As we explore the depths of ourselves, in other words, we find the experience that allows us gradually to understand something of God Himself. The sense of meaning that emerges from this experience is not easily defined because it cannot be summed up rationally, and it is not just something in the realm of emotions. It is in the order of personal experiencing, the way we understand on several levels what it means to belong to a family, or to be in love.

Believing, a Function of the Whole Person

Believing—and accepting the mystery of existence as it is—can only be done with and through the wholeness of ourselves. Belief is a dynamic function of the person, not just of the intellect or of the heart. When persons profess their beliefs, they say something about what they do in and through the complex unity of their personalities; they also acknowledge the spiritual significance and orientation given them in faith's native language of myth and symbol.

Believing forever involves us in questions not because of some human reluctance to believe but because it is through questions that we make our way forward into the deeper water of existence. In order to believe more firmly, we must constantly test the explanations delivered to us on the fine edges of our life experiences. Only the somnolent believer fails to ask questions and lives a life of faith from a shuttered telegraph station that no longer receives or sends messages.

Settling for security is the death of inquiry and therefore closing time for any active believing. Security ends disturbing thoughts, of course, and excuses us from examining our motives or recasting our religious symbols, but it also blows out the flame of living faith. In fact, it imposes deadness on life's best invitations, which is hardly made up for by the seeming stability of an unquestioning acceptance of any one set formula of faith or explanation of life. For believers, security is always being surrendered as the price of living in a fuller and richer way.

Perhaps an analogy with a marriage contract will help; the problems are, in fact, not dissimilar. Some couples, in order to affect equality of relationship and to avoid the misunderstandings and other contingencies of living together, draw up elaborate contracts stating each party's rights and obligations. The contract settles most of the problems that plague less-precise arrangements. Security based on justice insures a kind of stability that minimizes the chances of hurt.

In marriages where a man and woman sincerely build their relationship on faith associated with love, such a contract would be out of place. They know that they give up a measure of stability by committing themselves to each other in a relationship that is fundamentally unpredictable. Its stability, however, is of another sort, quite different from that of a legally binding contract. It is built on belief in each other, the kind of commitment that strengthens us and makes us vulnerable at the same time.

Couples who want to grow in their love know that they cannot shut themselves off from questions or from the experiences of changes that are bound to occur because of illness, aging, or other processes. They live by a kind of faith that is enhanced by the explorations of self, which are demanded of a man and woman who must continually find new answers together. They experience life through their belief in each other and through their willingness to risk change and hurt in pursuit of greater truth and depth together. It is the same way for questioning believers; the search keeps them alive and responsive, even though it forces them to live on the quivering edge of doubt and self-exploration.

What Churches Do That
We Can't Do by Ourselves

Many persons do not formalize their day-to-day difficulties in terms of generalized theological questions; they must deal with them on the level at which they meet them and give the best answers they can. It is difficult for most hard-working people to get very far in self-reflection or to draw much consolation or insight from the prophetic arts. They are too up against mortgages, sick children, and self-doubt to do much more, in the welter of everyday activity, than the best they can with the hope and prayer that it is the right thing.

This rather general state of affairs makes the challenge and opportunity of organized religion all the more significant. The churches are meant to supply the symbols and rituals that cut across the fatigue and confusion of life to deliver redemptive spiritual messages if not detailed meaning to ordinary persons. The marvelous work of organized religion is to provide the environment of active faith that speaks in many languages beyond logic of the religious significance and value of living.

The churches fill the role of wise and skilled counselors who know how to listen to even the slightest cry or least aspiration of human hearts and to respond with the words, images, liturgies, and relationships that say, in effect, "You and your life are understandable; what you long for makes sense. Read and recognize the story of your life in what the Lord teaches. Take strength from his promises."

Churches do not, in other words, preach or celebrate things that take people away from their struggles; they proclaim the religious reality of what people already experience. This is the kind of lively faith that makes it possible for persons whose lives may be splintered by a thousand cares to see themselves whole again. Such a living faith also underscores the moments and the values of existence that are truly redemptive.

Average persons keep faith by bringing themselves as honestly and truly as they can to the mostly undramatic but steadily demanding problems of living. The church, much as it does in witnessing the reality of marriage in the promises man and woman make to each other, constantly witnesses the saving realities of everyday life, pointing to and celebrating the incidents of trial and growth, the deaths and resurrections, through which we redeem ourselves and each other.

Saints Anonymous

The basic themes of the ordinary life have always existed; Jesus preaches their deepest meaning in his words and life. He reveals the profundity of our existence for us. We are strangers no more because we now possess the Spirit to illumine the faith significance of being human. The true impulse of church renewal is to draw back together the substance of life and faith, to make existence whole again by proclaiming the unity of our human and spiritual experiences.

The test of belief for average persons has always been in how they live rather than in how distinctly they recite the articles of the creed. There is, in other words, something always unconscious and unsymbolized about the lives of believers. They do not always know quite what they are doing, except that they are trying to do what is true and right. Just as the best kind of love is that which is unstudied and spontaneous, so the best kind of belief is not planned but comes to life in the moments that call for faithfulness and fidelity, for being responsive to the best possibilities in ourselves and in others. Formal faith helps us to recognize the deeper meaning of our homely efforts to invest ourselves truthfully in life; it validates them and strengthens us to continue giving our best to the unfolding mystery of our own incarnations.

Most people are so pressed with immediate concerns that they do not think very clearly or in much detail about whether they are being faithful or religious in dealing with these difficulties. Often enough, the persons who are self-consciously religious—pious might be a better word—destroy their own capacity for spontaneity and take the living quality out of what they call faith. Such, for example, are the do-gooders who are nice to you, not so much because of yourself but because they profess to see Christ in you. This is the classic illustration of behaving religiously in the best way for the wrong reason. Faith is not something conjured up to justify responding to persons in need; it inheres in the very response we make to the needy around us. We are faithful when we make ourselves present for the sake of others rather than for an invented reason that makes faithfulness extrinsic to human experience. People need the confirmation of their best instincts that religion affords as it puts into italics the experiences that are genuinely redemptive. Religion does not add redemptive meaning to these; it recognizes and celebrates it where it truly is.

Average individuals may be more aware of their needs than anything else. Life consists in getting through the activities and demands of the day with at least some minimal sense that we have kept our promises to each other and to the truth of ourselves. This is the small miracle of everyday living. It will not be noted if your cause for being declared a saint is ever formally introduced in Rome. But, of course, only a few saints are officially declared as such, compared to the millions of them all around us—Saints Anonymous, so to speak.

Believing for Saints Anonymous includes doing a decent job, being sensitive to one's family, and following the dictates of one's conscience. It extends to wanting to be loved and trying to love at the same time, of wanting to be fair and to be treated fairly as well. Each day can be like every other one, unless faith identifies those human exchanges in which we, in fact, work out our salvation together. People acquire a certain measure of wisdom, knowing, for example, that other people can hurt you, that they can be mean and small, and that even those you love can disappoint you.

Average men and women live with debts and taxes, with things they cannot control, and problems to which they wish that they did not have to pay any attention. They are surrounded at times by cruelties and injustices, by multiplied unfairnesses that make them wonder more than ever just what life, with broken promises and sudden deaths, with loose ends and unfulfilled hopes, really is all about.

It is in lives where persons are clearly aware of these problems that faith is already a living reality. The more we are committed to other persons, to achieving certain honorable goals, or to improving the world in some way, the more we are, whether we know it or not, active believers. Faith is something like the soul of life, the animating and energizing quality that makes existence possible. The capacity to believe processes experiences, enabling persons to reach each other, develop communities, and to enlarge the human sense of their own spirits and destinies. It is activated in all the difficult circumstances of life where gaps seem to exist in reasonableness and justice, in those incidents where evil abounds and persons are treated shamefully.

Believing is the only response adequate to the constant sacrileges committed against humanity. It is what men and women must do against all odds in order to give birth to a new and better future.

Faith has a creative function for human persons, because through it they can, even in the most desperate situations, renew themselves and others; the old prayer to the Holy Spirit is fulfilled in these people who daily renew the face of the earth.

Because men and women must believe—must, in other words, keep committing themselves to some interpretive framework in order to survive—the content of that framework is crucial. What we believe is decisive about the quality of our lives or the depths of our achievements. If, for example, beliefs are so diluted that they barely nourish or encourage us, we will have a difficult time facing up to the difficult questions that parade before us every day.

If the human person is nothing but an intricate machine, if all there is to believe in is efficiency, pleasure, or taking care of oneself, then belief itself is as restricted as a tape-winged dove; it cannot feel the throb of its power or its possibilities. That is why it is so important to associate religious faith with the richest possibilities of human personality. In a very real sense, the content of religious faith must help persons to believe in their own possibilities, to see past their faults to the self-transcending experiences of which they are capable.

Casting Our Nets into the Deep

One of the extraordinary aspects of the teachings of Jesus is found in his telling men and women that they can rise above the vindictiveness and estrangement that fill their lives when they do not keep faith with each other. He says there are yet resources of healing and self-realization that can be called upon if a person believes deeply enough. The content of the Christian Gospel bids us always to go deeper into ourselves and our experience, to find the kingdom within ourselves, in the powers that we can draw on to achieve what St. John describes as "life to the full."

That is not the power of positive thinking but the much harder task of finding and bringing the undiscovered aspects of our identities into being. Only a faith whose content recognizes and symbolizes the fact that men and women can always find fuller lives—only that faith can ever make them whole.

Faith is intimately involved in the human story, and religious faith takes us more deeply into it rather than farther away from it. The eyes of faith permit us to see ourselves as we are—and the selves we can yet be. It is the spark that dances across these flash points of experience all the days of our lives. Faith, then, is far from a frozen set of dogmas, and it has little resemblance to wishful thinking. Faith, insofar as it organizes us and orients us to what is really happening in and around us, situates us in reality rather than in some escapist illusion about life.

Faith in the Eternal Is Worked out in Time

First of all, faith roots us in time, in that strange indefinable experience that can be alternately perceived as an enemy or a friend. Faith does not merely espy the timeless world to come; it does something quite different because it alerts us to our meaning in time rather than just outside of it. Faith, in a certain sense, confronts us with time as an unalterable and yet profound condition of our self-realization and redemption. As psychologist Henri Yaker has observed:

> Men are called to redeem the contents of life in life, to salvage life by working in time until the final time, to find meaning by making each hour of life a theo-temporal hour, through decision rather than relying upon a cosmic transformation of nature. Not to be found in wind, hurricanes, and storms, Yahweh is to be found in history, where men

can read the beginning by the end, rather than the other way around.

Believing activity, in other words, involves us in ransoming our own time constantly through our acceptance of it as the medium in and through which we sense and touch each other's lives. Faith forces us to deal with time, and it never excuses us from this task. No mystical vision of eternity or of a world beyond time was ever granted to anyone who was not, first of all, clearly anchored in his or her own time or age. Faith, the act through which we make ourselves present to reality as it is and we are, provides the basis for the other rich and complex responses through which we best respond to time as a condition of life.

The latter are, of course, hope and love, each of which enables us to deal with the temporal condition of our lives in a constructive manner. Through hope and love we do, in fact, redeem our times by operationally living out the vision of meaning and values supplied by faith. Believing inserts us in meaningful time because it lights up the significance of the human community and builds the foundations for the experiences through which we touch each other's lives redemptively.

Faith alters our time sense; it does not just manipulate or distort it the way a drug might. We experience time more fully because we see the world and ourselves more clearly by the light of its revelation. Now is the time of salvation, the Bible tells us, and so it is for the believer who understands that only as we enter into the demanding processes that take their shape in time, do we lay hold of our deepest sense of our eternal destinies. The believer becomes a hoper and a lover in the gritty world of time and space. That is where we sense the mysteries with which we must deal if we are going to be true believers.

The Complexities of Being Human

These include the strange mystery of ourselves, for example, and the many layers of our experiences that we must befriend in some way before we can possess or become ourselves. The problem is that we need a sense of our own possibilities of growth, a vision of what we can become, if we are going to face the complex and ambivalent strands of our own identity.

Faith provides that vision because it acknowledges the roiling primitive qualities within us while it enables us to temper and integrate these as part of our true selves. That is how faith makes us whole, by making it possible for us to face the evil inside of us and not to be overcome by it. The men or women who remain unacquainted with the dark sides of themselves are strangers to their real identities. Belief has the power to fuse these complex energies so that they may serve rather than betray the unique individual personality.

Faith gives us a good look at ourselves when its dimensions of potential meaning are large and strong enough to accept the human personality in all its flawed majesty. Any vision of supposed faith that deliberately truncates or automatically rules out certain parts of our experiences harms us more than it helps us. Such, as the late psychologist Rollo May has noted, are the images of the noble savage or the totally good young who can only be corrupted from the outside. This generates what May termed a "pseudo-innocence" because such individuals never identify or come to terms with the other very real and very powerful aspects of their personalities. They fail to achieve those identities that are based on their complex internal realities; they do not know how to use aggression or other strong feelings constructively. Their faith in themselves, their fellow human beings, and God is restricted because they have neither seen nor understood the full truth about themselves.

Faith Makes Us Whole

Faith serves an integrating function because it does not flinch at what it finds in our ambivalence or narcissistic self-concern. It provides us with the view of reaching beyond these, using their strengths for the richer purposes of serving and loving others. Persons faithful to themselves possess power—the power of the Spirit—to harness their passions positively. They can believe in themselves because they are not surprised at anything about themselves, and they know that their development is never perfect or finished with.

They must keep believing, in other words, to keep themselves together in a healthy dynamic way; their believing sums them up, good and bad, in discernible identities. That, of course, is the kind of person in whom others can also believe, in whom they spontaneously believe because such a person is already available to them in a rich and true manner.

Deceit, defensiveness, the manipulation of appearances: All of these are used to get responses from people. They may get a species of acquiescence, a shallow response, but it is nothing like the kind of faith we invest in people who are trustworthy, precisely because their faults—and therefore their depths—are not hidden.

This life-oriented belief allows us to deal with our guilt as well as the myriad anxieties that accompany us through life. The achievement of healthy self-esteem depends on establishing a truthful relationship to ourselves. If we are horrified by the discoveries we make about our capacities to fall short of an ideal, we will never be comfortable with or confident in ourselves. The faith that understands the human condition, inlaid as it is with imperfections, enables us to face and forgive ourselves for the sometimes jumbled psychological inheritance within us. It is precisely this shambling and faulted self that we must believe in if we are going to live what we call the Christian life.

If we can accept and confront ourselves as sinners—or at least as psychologically imperfect—then we can begin to do something in and through our own true personalities. We are, in a brief definition, believing sinners who through faith find the strength to forgive and heal and love. That is what the life of faith is all about—redeeming ourselves through the promises Jesus gave us when he took on the human condition.

Faith, a Moveable Feast

The process aspect of living faith—the way this is accomplished—involves us in something we would avoid completely if we were terrorized by our shortcomings. The central, mystical, and transforming experience of faith asks us to let others see the truth of ourselves, to reveal, in other words, precisely what we are afraid people will find out—who and what we really are.

This dynamic, as mentioned earlier, places us at that point of necessary but easy convergence between what has been called natural and supernatural faith. The processes are indistinguishable and can be recognized as aspects of the same phenomenon when we believe enough in ourselves and others to let them see us as we are. This transaction changes us, exorcising the demons within by taking away their selfish destructive power and freeing us to become more of our true selves at the same time. It is also a reciprocal process because, as we reveal ourselves, so the other responds with a greater revelation of his or her truth.

People have to believe in each other in order to enter into this experience—and they deepen their belief through the process itself. We know even as we are known in the experience that allows us some insight into the faithful person's dynamic and reciprocal relationship with God. Knowing and being known counterpoint the faith experience of life, allowing us to deal with our tangled personal truths, to redeem and give wholeness to each other, and to sense the reality beyond us of which these are both the image and the echo.

Chapter Eight

Creative Faith

Creeds are easy, unless you are a philosopher who agonizes over the working of a particular clause. The recital of the creed gives us a sense of security and makes us feel comfortable and approved by the church itself. We are so habituated to the doctrinal summation through a lifetime of repetition that we may be dulled to the more exciting and confronting aspects of living faith.

I do not believe that you can make an act of faith in the mysteries of the God-head in other than a living and changing manner. We are the ones who live and change, of course, and our faith is constantly shifting and expanding in order to accommodate the pressures of its own developing complexity. William James, the famous psychologist, once said that we believe all that we can, and we would believe everything if only we could. The human person is a believer but not in a naïve or easy manner; as men and women mature they must believe more and take more risks and more deep breaths in the process. As we grow older we find that life is not exactly what we thought it was, and although we may therefore feel betrayed or at least surprised, we can neither turn back nor look away without betraying ourselves even more.

Believing makes adults out of us when we have to search our reservoirs of faith for the understandings and symbols to explain wickedness, tragedy, and the failure of love. This does not require us to hold on to a child's version of the universe but actively to search out an adult's understanding of it.

Faith Is Not a Tranquilizer

This is the part that is difficult because, quite against our expectations that religious faith will calm our inner seas, we discover that it leads us into brisker winds and more towering storm clouds. Faith does not pull us apart, but neither does it set us apart from what all men and women must face once they awaken to the mysterious challenges of becoming human. These include many elements, from the loss of their first innocence about the sun-filled world of childhood to the last tasks of old age in which life, like an unbraiding rope, can seem to come apart before they have even had a good look at it.

The developing person becomes more aware of his or her own complexity through all of this, especially in the area of human relationships that seem to be self-entangling and almost too painful to speak the truth about. This sense of a differentiated and nonsimple self is further weighted with a sense of the dreams and longings we have shared with all those who have lived before us and who, in some way, seem to live in us still. How do persons get enough room even to see themselves clearly for a moment, much less to grasp theirs or the world's meaning?

A simple and old-fashioned faith may seem the right answer to the questions without answers that gradually pile up in the minds of sensitive persons. This works for some, although it is not certain that they are more blessed because of that. Such a faith may shut their eyes against the landscape of life so that they do not know its terrors, but they miss its beauty as well. Believing persons need a religious faith that opens them to, even when it cannot fully explain, the contradictions and sometimes nonlinear quality of human experience.

Believing is more like sailing on uncharted seas than staying in port telling tales of the demons over the horizon. Sailing is not a glass-sea sport; only the individual ready to harness the invisible wind can ride the cauldron successfully. Faith does not make the journey easy; it does, however, make it possible and, at each succeeding stage, meaningful. I believe, in other words, that religious faith is made for living life rather than for hiding away from it. It must, therefore, be capable of sustaining us as we grow, become puzzled, hurt, and finally transformed by the whirling and flashing experiences of life.

Faith Is Not a Fixative

Faith is not a preservative; it does not fix explanations that last, in any one form, for a lifetime. Faith is something alive, a dynamic that related us to the shifting nature of ourselves and our world. It is creative of ourselves and of our individual meaningful experiences of life. Believing involves us in a process that is endlessly repeated for each of us and is never fully completed for any of us.

The essential notes of what it means to believe are best understood if we look at the creative process itself. This helps to illumine what I believe in about belief and also allows us to appreciate the manner in which we know deep within us the basic rhythm of the Christian view of life.

This catches what Jesus meant when he spoke of our need to have the faith of little children. It is the unspoiled vision of the child that must be available to creative persons if they are to break out of prefabricated existences and bring something new into the world. The child has a vision of the possible about things; this is the same vision creative persons employ as they look at problems or work toward deeper insights.

Faith's Subject: The Possible

The vision of the possible is precisely what faith restores to us so that we can, in fact, get up in the morning or return to tasks and relationships that would otherwise break us under their deadening weight. This refocus on the possible—on all that is fresh and yet to be—is a healthy impulse through which we let go of something of ourselves in order to lay hold of something richer and better.

The basic experience of creative artists of any kind involves them in a dying to themselves in order to bring a new vision of the possible into existence. This is not something that creative persons can plan or induce; it is in the order of response to what they can see in life. Believing is just such an experience because it continually challenges us to look at life and, even at the price of death to an old way of looking at things, to respond with behavior that springs from the level of possibility rather than cliché. That cannot be planned, and it is only faintly memorialized by reciting various creeds; it is something demanding a reorganization of ourselves in accordance with a lively vision rather than a happy memory.

Poets speak of learning to "throw themselves away" in the creative process, of having to surrender themselves in order to bring an enlarged self to life. They experience a certain disorganization of their adjustment in view of this newer and higher level of integration. They suffer what the late psychologist Frank Barron called an experience of "diffusion" in order to be able to come together again in the achievements of their creations.

Creators re-create themselves, one might say, even as believers, facing the changing and difficult contours of their experiences, must, in the very act of believing, disorganize themselves and bring themselves together around the vision of possibilities that their faith makes available to them. In this way faith makes us whole, not by cementing us in some former set toward life, but by breaking us open continuously so that we can be reintegrated at a higher level with a deepened sense of ourselves and of the meaning of our lives. This is the mystic realm of religious experience, and it has a face as plain and simple as everyday life in which we die daily, not through stoic mortification but through creative living.

The very word creative has been cheapened in our culture, and it may be difficult to grasp it again as the most profoundly descriptive word that we have about the life of faith. That is why we work out our salvation in fear and trembling rather than in safety and security; the creative strength of believing is manifest in the conditions of uncertainty and ambivalence that mark our days. We are meant to respond to each other on the risky edge of living where only those with a vision of the possible are capable of giving new life to each other.

Incarnation, Death, Resurrection

As Frank Barron noted in his description of the creative artist's work,

> [T]he individual is willing to "die unto himself," i.e., to permit an achieved adaptation or state of relative equilibrium to perish. And there are no guarantees that something better will thereby be arrived at. Looking back-wards from the end point of the creative process, we are inclined to say, "Ah, yes, it had to be so; the chance had to be taken; the chalice could not be passed; the agony was necessary for the redemption and the resurrection." But facing forward in time we see only

risk and difficulty, and if we have not the courage to endure diffusion ("suffer death") we cannot achieve the new and more inclusive integration ("gain the light").

Ordinary persons are immersed in a life that challenges them to be creative in their own ways, to leave their marks not on a statue or a poem but on those they love or teach or just stand by in hard times. Creativity for most of us is not taking a ceramics class in evening school as much as it is facing into every day with a vision of its promises and a willingness to die to something of ourselves in order to redeem these.

The psychological reality of the process is lighted up by, but not radically different from, the struggle of the writer or the sculptor. What is striking, of course, is how these dynamics parallel the life theme of all of Jesus' teachings. We are given life not to hoard it or to protect it but to invest it through committing ourselves, at the risk of suffering, to recreating the face of the earth.

The work of the Spirit is surely that of the faith we profess: to take on our flesh, that is, our own identities, and to suffer the deaths that are the necessary condition for our resurrecting ourselves and others with new life. We keep faith by responding with our total selves to this most fundamental of all religious experiences, the daily round of living and loving that defines life for most of us.

How Are We Born Again?

It has always seemed to me that the questioning Nicodemus, wondering how a man could be born again, was staring, with only a stirring of comprehension at the possibilities of the faith life that Jesus was preaching to him. "How can a man be born again?" That is indeed a profound and bewildering inquiry because it raises the vision that believing in Jesus enables us to re-create ourselves, to return after our failures to a renewed sense of our possibilities with each other.

Ordinary life is not supplanted but fulfilled by the regenerating power through which we can meet again after we have injured each other with the creative and redemptive faith that enables us to see what we can be once more. What is Christian forgiveness from the heart if not the restoration of our possibilities? We are continually born again—and not just metaphorically—through our faith in Jesus. That belief enables us to recognize the essential features of life, to see deeply into them as the human raw material of our redemption, much as the artist's creative eye allows him to see deeply into the changing colors of a sunset or the beauty in the tired faces of homeward-bound commuters.

Faith enables us to see what is already there in a fresh manner and to give our best energies to it every day. We are born again by reaching toward each other across the crooked ways and mounted entanglements of daily life.

Salvation: A Function of Our Relationships

Jesus, in responding to Nicodemus, seems to say this clearly as he concludes, "he who acts in truth comes into the light, to make clear that his deeds are done in God" (John 3:21). Belief in the Lord, in other words, provides the vision of the human situations and responses that are redemptive transactions. Faith lights these up and enables us to recognize the values that are the foundations of the kingdom. Creative believing always gives life, but it is not a sweet or easy exercise. Being born again is a difficult task, and it is only accomplished by those who learn to face the hurts and deaths that are implicit in finding and rooting out what is selfish in ourselves so that our own truths can emerge more clearly.

There is a lot of dying in forgiving others or in allowing them to forgive us for the way we can misunderstand and mistreat each other in life. If we could not be born again, if we could not return to a sense of our possibilities—the very thing that creative faith enables us to do—we would be the most desperate of persons. It was well said by Paul that without the power of the Resurrection our faith would be vain and our human state pitiable.

Jesus does not point away from but squarely at our lives as the setting in which we save and are saved through believing. I am indebted to a scripture scholar colleague, the late Father John Mc-Govern, for a reminder of how directly Jesus draws us back to a sharpened sense of our true selves in Luke's Gospel. Luke 9:51 to 19:28, in what the late Jesuit Father John L. McKenzie has termed the "conscious art" of Luke, is an extended manual for Christian believers. This journey narrative presents Jesus moving into his future, his journey into the eschaton, the age of Christ, and the age of all Christians.

We find powerful insights into the human dimensions of believing stated within this tension-giving setting of Jesus on the way to the accomplishment of his life work. At the very start, four themes emerge that allow us to understand what we must face in ourselves and in life if we are to make the journey of faith with him. We read of four human encounter situations that describe essential characteristics of believing disciples. They underscore rather than override experiences that we can all recognize very clearly:

> They entered a Samaritan town to prepare for his passing through, but the Samaritans would not welcome him because he was on his way to Jerusalem. When his disciples James and John saw this, they said, "Lord, would you not have us call down fire from heaven to destroy them?" He turned toward them only to reprimand them. (Luke 9:52–56)

Jesus points to the strength we need to be nonviolent in the believing life. This can only arise in the lives of those who have come to terms with themselves and the shadowed side of their personalities. It is easy to hurt and to be vengeful, but it is far more difficult to temper one's hostile impulses in the perspective of a larger and more understanding view of life. Believers, in other words, do not act only on their immediate feelings of the moment because they can see beyond the instant to a broader purpose that is poorly served by anger and the desire to get even. The passage recognizes our human capacity for destructive violence and singles it out as something that must die if we are to re-create the face of the earth.

Followers of Jesus are ever ready, then, to understand and forgive both themselves and others, a process that requires more than diplomacy and tact. It demands a steady transformation of ourselves and a willingness to surrender small and easy victories in view of making ourselves present in a truly healing way in life. Believers are not strangers to their own humanity; they have achieved a wholeness that does not naïvely ignore our potential evil but chooses to subordinate and defuse this in view of a more patient and understanding approach to humankind. Violence is one of our easiest temptations; to be determinedly nonviolent in order to be understanding is a foundation stone of the unabstracted life of faith.

> As they were making their way along, someone said to him, "I will be your follower wherever you go." Jesus said to him, "The foxes have lairs, the birds of the sky have nests, but the Son of Man has nowhere to lay his head." (Luke 9:57–58)

Jesus points to a central human problem that is related to our capacity to respond creatively in life. Persons must find their own centers, their own substantial identities, as the anchor points in the shifting and insecure environment of life. Individuals may listen to many voices within themselves—and to many more in the world beyond them—but, in the last analysis, they must live out of their own depths or they fail to live truly at all. Believers, in other words, must examine and test their beliefs against experiences, opening rather than closing themselves continually to the teeming contradictions of life, not depending on fads or rumors, but on the purified sense of the inner self that is thereby achieved.

No Belief without Self-Knowledge

Our personal identities—knowing who we are as individuals—are, therefore, not a luxury but a prerequisite for the life of faith. We can only believe in and through our own personalities, or our signatures of faith are counterfeit. It is not possible to believe maturely merely on the strength of somebody else's persuasion; that is, of course, the perennial danger attached to enthusiastic but not necessarily very deep religious movements. Faith does not obliterate our identities; rather it builds on them, giving a blessing to every sincere effort to bring the truth of ourselves and the richness of our unique gifts into being.

> To another he said, "come after me." The man replied, "Let me bury my father first." Jesus to him, "Let the dead bury their dead; come away and proclaim the kingdom of God." (Luke 9:59–60)

In this passage, frequently moralized into thoughts about filial piety, Jesus points to a deep and abiding issue that the believer must confront and deal with in life. Indeed, it is one of the most difficult problems that can be faced by persons because it centers on the conflict of loyalties that is inevitable in the human situation. The believer must be able to recognize rather than deny the conflicts, many of which are rooted in patterns of life that are self-enclosing. This is true in something as familiar as the merger of separate families through the marriage of two of their members.

The clash of traditions and of simple ways of doing things generates tension in many a household. It is very hard for any of us to detach ourselves from our own heritages without disowning them, to make room for another in our life-space without absorbing them totally in our lifestyle. Selfishness closes us over, making us view the world systematically in terms of our own self-interest. This bony ring of self-concern chokes us to death because, whether in reference to us as individuals, families, or peoples, it convinces us that there is only one way to do something, and that is our way. The believer must grow in what psychologist Gordon Allport once described as the process of de-centering ourselves. This requires a willingness to die, which leads to the resurrection experience of resolving differences and respecting persons of different backgrounds and outlooks.

The first step in breaking free of our own cramped vision of the universe is the recognition that we will experience tension in admitting and working out the divided loyalties of our lives. It is an ongoing process that measures the breadth and depth of our Christian vision. Nobody can escape this sharply honed dimension of personal growth, which insistently asks that we discover new possibilities of response and affirmation within ourselves. The believer who does not recognize this as an essential component of the faith response is dealing with a dead rather than a living faith.

> Yet another said to him, "I will be your follower, Lord, but first let me take leave of my people at home." Jesus answered him, "Whoever puts his hand to the plow but keeps looking back is unfit for the reign of God." (Luke 9:61–62)

In an era during which so many persons have longed for what seems to have been a simpler past, including the Reformers of the Reform, this statement of the Lord's is a forthright and strong invitation to be decisive in the present in view of the future, to live now for the world that is just coming into being. Religious nostalgia is as tempting an invitation as any other form of retrospective longing, and many people, worn down by the strain of renewal and its transformations, wish for a restoration of what were at least more secure good old days.

Faith as Discovery

Jesus challenges any such inclinations with this response, which reminds believers of their essential orientations toward the discovery and creativity of a new age. The person of faith does more than remember or mourn what has gone before. Belief opens us to what can be if we have the courage to let go of our past because of our Christian realization that we are builders of the future. Believing Christians take on responsibility for their decisions, understanding the risk implicit in each one and moving with them toward the future to which they give shape.

Contemporary America is fascinated with the future; nobody is more committed to it than the man or woman of faith who actively attempts to make it a place in which the human family can realize its destiny more fully. The late B. F. Skinner was absolutely correct in saying that we cannot scare people into preparing for a better future; the Christian vision of the Gospel offers us the sense of direction and the guarantees we need in order to build it in a positive and hopeful manner. That takes a living commitment to things we have not yet seen or heard, to the possibilities of people whose faces we will never see, to the next things more than the last things.

Near the end of the musical play and movie, *1776*, a discouraged John Adams, having arrived early in the room where the divided colonial delegates have been meeting, steps toward the front of the darkened stage and poses a question to the audience. "Is anybody there? Does anybody care?" he asks plaintively, "Does anybody see what I see?"

In many ways, modern men and women peering into the darkness of their futures ask the same questions. Is anybody there? Does anybody care? These are the searching inquiries that make believers examine themselves in terms of the qualities listed by Luke in his narrative. The believer must hear the questions of contemporary men and women and respond with the faith that does not necessarily answer all their wonders but which at least helps to frame them in appropriate human theological terms.

The church stands there, its spires against the darkness, not so much as a symbol of its past as a sign of its living concern for the future. Believing is operative and functional in history but only when believers are alive to their own capacities to breathe on others and to resurrect them, to give them back their possibilities, to give the human family its future. Is anybody there? Does anybody care? Does anybody see what I see? Only we believers can give the answers to these haunting questions.

Chapter Nine

What Do I Believe In?

The question is fair enough, but it is a question that cannot be answered fully in intellectual terms, perhaps not in any terms. Believing is an activity that arises from many levels of our beings. Some of these we recognize; others we glimpse only fleetingly; still others we never sense at all. Believing is something we do with all of ourselves; it can never be summed up in intellectual statements alone, howsoever worthy these may be. It is relatively easy to recite the creed and to think we have accomplished a religious action.

The test of the creed is, however, in life, as it always has been. That is something that involves more than our minds, and we can only explore it with practical theological questions like, "Why do I get up in the morning?" "How do I love my friends and enemies?" and "Why do I live the life that I do?" Something as personal as believing requires personal answers.

The Kingdom Is within Us

Faith is a dynamic process—a living part of ourselves—that is redemptive and creative of life and through which we recognize the religious nature of the adventurous pilgrimage we are on together. Jesus came to point toward those parts of life in which operative faith yields a renewing wholeness of meaning.

The church is meant to be creative in its own commitment to this living faith, and the last thing it needs to fear is the inevitable dying that is the price of a fuller realization of itself. It is understandable that the church—or that those who administer it—is keenly aware of its structures and traditions, but these are meant to house a living and sometimes squabbling family of believers rather than an obedient and loyal regiment. Faith, like creative energy, is meant to be expended rather than conserved.

Jesus, then, is not just a great man or a distant historical character but a living presence who reveals both the Father and the meaning of our lives to us. If we examine our lives, I think we can see the experiences through which we redeem ourselves through redeeming each other. We live in a continuing mystery of His own existence and come to face and know for ourselves the great moments of meeting and sharing and separating through which we express the faith that continually re-creates and therefore resurrects us.

We can feel that in the tensions of being true to ourselves that are found not in dramatic incidents but in familiar events, like keeping a promise or being an honest friend or being faithful to somebody we love. Something dies and something new comes to life in us when we make a free and open entrance into these believing moments. They are scattered throughout every day, the raw material of redemption that is processed creatively by living faith.

The Church, More a Laboratory Than a Museum

The church, then, is not an authoritarian institution with all the answers; it has never been very believable in that guise anyway or, for that matter, true to itself. The church does much better by itself and by people when, like the creative person, it "throws itself away" in an ever-fresh redemptive commitment to the people of the world. To do this it must allow some of its crustier defenses to die and to reveal its mystery and wisdom more freely.

Christ's church is surely meant to be a creative force rather than a fixative in human history. The remarkable thing is that it has such enormous creative resources at its disposal for accomplishing the primary task of symbolizing and celebrating the central redemptive aspects of life. Instead of treating its human and symbolic wealth gingerly, or with a banker's view to control, the church can freely spend its resources and only find them re-created as a result.

Many observers have noted that the search for contemporary religious symbols and myths—the very language faith lives on—is one of our most urgent quests. We need to speak to human experience in those symbolic terms and stories that enable the person to find his way through the wasteland and back to a sense of himself. This primarily occurs through the work of creative theologians and liturgists who can sense the religious truths that need to be expressed in fresh ways and who need encouragement and support to do it for us. These are people who, like all true creators, move into the darkness, not self-conscious about their movements but sure of their sense of direction. These creative believers discover and hold up for the rest of us the symbols that bind our faith and experiences together.

If there was ever a time when we needed healthy creativity in the service of believing man, it is surely now. The temptation, of course, is to keep these people under control lest they disturb something called tradition. A misapplied sense of tradition, however, is precisely what dulls our senses to the truths we desperately need to live by; we need a new way of seeing the profoundly religious nature of our everyday experiences. Only the creative persons—

and by this I do not mean the bizarre and pseudo-creative individuals who sometimes pass themselves off as the real thing—can dip into the hidden levels of their own consciousnesses as well as that of the human race. They understand the language of faith in a way that allows them to translate it so that we can all comprehend and speak it better ourselves.

Standing out of the Spirit's Light

This is not luxury or a fascinating and colorful hobby for some interested people; it is a necessity if we are to meet the demands of the human need to believe. The trouble is that you cannot give orders to or supervise the work of creative persons; you can only, as Alexander the Great learned from Diogenes, stand out of their light.

No wonder creative persons have so often had difficulties with organized religion; it has always tried to harness forces that can only flow freely. Critics of creative people, imagining them to be an untidy and vaguely Bohemian group, forget the intrinsic demands of the authentic act of creation. It demands everything—that "throwing away of the self"—if it is to be successful. As Barron noted, "the artist submits his will to a purpose beyond himself in a manner complete enough for the humblest monk."

The people who function creatively in theology, especially in its pastoral and liturgical dimensions, should be given as much encouragement as possible at the present time because of what they can do for us in supplying the religious symbolism to nourish our faith. This can be done by no one else. Creative persons do not, in a profound and wonderful sense, know what they are doing; they know how to do it and they know the price of self-surrender that they must pay in order to be successful. It is the instinct of organizers to ask for five-year plans and projections; these are, of course, what creative persons cannot seriously offer at all.

Regrettably, the Reform of the Reform does not trust healthy creativity but, branding all experimentation as wild and dangerous, is trying mightily to control the liturgy in an absolute manner once more, fitting it for the straitjacket of Latin and denying the opportunity for local churches to mine the riches of their own symbols in worship. Do they trust the Spirit if they do not trust healthy creative theologians and liturgists? Only truly creative believers can find their way forward in the sound liturgical development that parallels sound theological development. These creative liturgists and theologians find the way for the rest of us at the same time.

Picasso was once asked to explain the work of the artist, and in probably as good an answer as he could give, he replied, "To make." When asked just how this process worked, he responded, "Don't talk to the driver!"

Recreating the Face of the Earth

I believe in visions but not those of saints from other times as much as those of the persons of creative faith and temperament who help us to see our way into the Space/Information Age. These visions of our possibilities, cast in the forms and symbols that speak to us now, are indispensable for the vigor of our faith life in Jesus. These creative visionaries are building the church anew, giving a rebirth to the lifestyle and sacramental reality of the believing community. They help us to recognize ourselves and each other as well as our ever-fresh opportunities to heal and resurrect each other. The Reform of the Reform may successfully stop their work, but they impede the re-creation of the face of the earth at the same time.

I think we should believe in these theologians and liturgists enough to allow them to make mistakes or occasionally to be obscure in the way they try to speak to us. The final test—and the one we can trust completely—is in the response of the believing community to the pastoral and liturgical forms they provide for us. If these capture the essence of the Gospel in our language, we respond with a new fullness to the religious nature of living; we believe more deeply and recognize the mystery of living in Jesus in the bread they break for us.

We need that believing community with its sure sense of what holds together in terms of its operational faith. I believe in the church, not only as mystery, but also as organization steeped in familiar strengths and weaknesses. We need an organized church to provide the identity for the community of fellow believers who can be so enormously supportive to us as we stand facing the struggles and problems of our individual lives.

Our faith needs the voices and the feel of people who believe in us and stay close to us on our long and seemingly lonely journeys. The sacraments are human signs that fit the stages of those journeys, and these would also be diminished, as would be our recognition of each other, without a gathering of believers to which we can join ourselves.

In this living community the richest treasures of the faith have always been generously passed on to others. To mention but one distinctive thing that can only be handed on through the spirit of a community, our senses of sin and its forgiveness constitute an important inheritance. We are born and grow among people with senses of how they can hurt each other as well as senses of how, through forgiveness and healing, they can restore that state of possibility that is so fundamental to a living and creative faith.

Related to this are the symbols and rituals that are important for the experiences of life. As mentioned before, these symbols, the discoveries of our most creative believers, sound a public, resonating tone for our most common religious quests; they enable us to recognize our kinship with each other and with all people who have preceded us or who will come after us. An organized church becomes an indispensable treasury for these, an appropriate housing for the signs and symbols of living faith as well as a home for the believers who feed on them.

Yes to an Institutional Church

An organized church also offers an identity and a unifying tradition for persons of very differing cultural and ethnic backgrounds. It provides a meeting ground on which they can recognize each other as human beings without sacrificing either their languages or their heritages. Only an institutional church offers us the transcending identity that enables us to continue to be different while we sense our deep unity in faith. If we are ever to help human beings to live as brothers and sisters—as well as put an end to elitism in religion—it will require something like an institutional church as a setting in faith for it.

In the same way, the office of pope offers us an invaluable symbol of unity, a sense of religious awareness that would be greatly diminished without him. There are layers of tradition that need to be peeled away from the papacy, but the core notion is one of theological and psychological genius; it also demands an institution to support it. In the same way, the organized church provides a forum for the dialogue of living in faith and, despite noises to the contrary, has a large capacity for allowing differences of outlooks as one of its greatest, if most underestimated, strengths.

These observations have been made about the structured church as something that I feel it is important to believe in. This goes counter to the opinion of many people who despair of an institutional church ever keeping up with the needs and experiences of its people. There is inevitable tension involved in keeping the organized church a believable phenomenon, but anyone who is seriously concerned about the religious future of humankind must also be concerned with this problem. We need to have faith in the church, a creative kind of faith that keeps turning it back to its possibilities and never lets it rest on its accomplishment or, God help us, on its authority.

The Church and Mystery

I believe in the experiences the church itself has singled out as essential for human development; freedom and trust and enough time to grow. These experiences are familiar to us, but they are seldom granted except by persons who believe enough in others to give these things away to them.

The greatest test of the church will always be how much it actually believes in the things it says are good, in the things it can only give away, in the things that persons need in order to be able to believe in themselves or in anyone else. These elements are as basic as air and water to the healthy development of human personality. Giving them away involves us in a transaction of faith because these things cannot be faked or otherwise produced artificially; people know the difference right away. Sacrilege might well be defined as that offense against persons that is committed by others who offer them the stone of manipulation for the bread of faith.

Fidelity is also an expression of the profound mystery through which we work out our salvation in relationship to each other. Only through a commitment to the best that is in ourselves and in the living experiences of good people do we ever forge our way past the letter of the law and begin to understand the Sprit who gives life to us all.

Fidelity, however, is sometimes fragile, and it is often under siege. It is the special test of how much we are willing to believe and of how many deaths we are willing to undergo in order to keep re-creating our lives afresh with each other.

True Christian can never be bored because they are always implicated in the new discoveries of personalities that are made only by passionate believers. Believing makes us look on each other as persons; maybe that says everything as briefly as it can be put. But it is not a simple charge to be nice or to do good and avoid evil. Looking on each other means to preserve a vision of what each of us can become—a perception of the possibilities that seem to be lost under the veil of our shortcomings or failures—and to keep working through those relationships by which we become ourselves. That is work enough for a lifetime, and even then it will be left unfinished. But belief concerns itself with what is unfinished about us and our world.

That is the crucial mystery at the heart of all our relationships, that arena in which we touch and are touched by any hints we will ever get about transcendent meaning. We must keep believing in each other in order to keep our relationships alive; love does not take care of itself, and lovers who fail to sense each other's changeableness will soon only remember or sadly mourn their love.

Life—a religious life, if you like—is worked through in the way we strive to be faithful and true and loving to each other. That is filled with numberless deaths and rebirths, with the strange and sometimes dizzying experiences that break us out of our own narcissistic jails and give us the chance to celebrate the freedom of God's children together. What use are the creeds without this? What meaning in life exists for the person who has been denied these experiences or who has learned to treat people either as temptations or as tasks to be carried out well in view of a celestial gold star?

Faith is not something to be hoarded in a miserly or in a fearful fashion. It is inadequate if it is considered only as the light by which we can see others and, through doing self-conscious good to them, add to our bank account of rewards in heaven. Many of us have been victims of this tendency to use faith as an instrument for securing our salvation; we view it, when we are so persuaded, as something that must be clutched and conserved and that cannot be spent freely and lovingly.

What Was It I Wanted to Be?

I am reminded of the old actor, James Tyrone, in Eugene O'Neill's famous play, *Long Day's Journey into Night*. He has been miserly all his life and now, with one son a drunk, and the other desperately sick with tuberculosis, and his wife a drug addict, he pauses as he tightens a light bulb he had unscrewed earlier in order to save money: "What the hell was it I wanted to buy, I wonder, that was worth . . . Well, no matter. It's a late day for regrets. . . . No, I don't know what the hell it was I wanted to buy."

Obsessive Christians, fearful of their faith, may find that they cannot quite remember what they were saving it for either. Humankind and the world—you and I—need to be believed in here and now, and only faith that is ready to spend itself without fear that it will exhaust itself is up to the job. Christians who timidly perform saving acts of virtue have not yet understood that they can buy neither happiness nor heaven in such a way.

I can imagine nothing sadder than supposed believers who kept all the good news to themselves, a marvelous orthodox store, and who now ask, in the tones of persons who feel they have missed life somewhere along the line, "What the hell was it I wanted to buy, I wonder, that was worth . . . Well, no matter. It's a late day for regrets."

Life and faith are grander than that truncated conception. The Gospels are the good news and we are barely at the beginning of understanding the person, not as the naked ape but as the believing animal who can be believed in. In the long run, that is why I get up in the morning and lead the life I do. I believe in the human person, and it is not an impossible fancy to think that God does too. It is important to try to understand the person and to provide the conditions needed to become fully grown. We are all caught up in the mystery of incarnation, in that long pilgrimage, plagued with darkness and misunderstood directions, by which we move toward the fullness of ourselves and the fullness of time. We are saved or lost depending on how much we give or withhold ourselves from each other along the way.

Love Fulfills All Commandments

I believe in love, not abstractly or wishfully, but because in my own life it has been the experience of love that has caused me to search myself most deeply and to sort out the things I believe in from the things I have believed about. Love sets you on a journey and then gradually transforms itself on you, bidding you to emerge more from yourself and to invest yourself more deeply in the life and concerns of another. The journey is, however, the thing; it leads away from living by expectations, pleasing others, or from thinking that faith is found only in ecclesiastical decrees or theological textbooks.

You can love and not examine what you believe in—but you cannot do it for long. You cannot, in fact, love and escape the taste of the deepest and most demanding mystery of the Gospel. That believing in Jesus is tested by our belief in each other and that anyone who believes and loves will find that his or her experience of life is thereby deepened and transformed. The bells of the scriptures ring clearly in your life when you try to love. What may once have been random events are now understood as the feasts and friendships, the loneliness and separation, the small deaths and resurrections through which we sense the mystery of Jesus in our own lives.

Life does not just happen to us, and as we become aware of our freedom, we grapple with the vexation of an endless series of increasingly difficult choices. The life of the Spirit is something we break into as we break out of ourselves through trying to love more deeply and truly. That is the creative choice that developing faith offers to us each day—to get better at throwing ourselves away—and to know that, finally, this is the way that, gloriously and in each other's company, we find out who we are.

References

Introduction

May, Rollo. *Power and Innocence: A Search for the Sources of Violence.* New York: W.W. Norton and Company, 1972.

Chapter 2

Bellah, Robert. *Beyond Belief.* New York: Harper and Row, 1970.

Campbell, Joseph. *Thou Art That: Transforming Religious Metaphor*, edited by Eugene Kennedy. Novato, CA: New World Library, 2002.

Frank, Jerome B. *Persuasion and Healing.* Baltimore: The Johns Hopkins Press, 1961.

Kennedy, Eugene. "Earthrise: The Dawning of a New Spiritual Awareness," *New York Times Magazine.* Interview with Joseph Campbell, April 1979.

Kuruvilla, Carol. "Bob Ballard, Explorer Who Found the Titanic, Now Says He May Have Found Evidence of Noah's Flood," *New York Daily News*, December 14, 2012.

O'Malley, John A. *What Happened at Vatican II.* Cambridge, MA.: The Belknap Press of Harvard University Press, 2008.

Chapter 3

Droege, Thomas A. "Developmental View of Faith," *Journal of Religion and Health* 11, no. 4, October 1972.

Erickson, Erick. *Childhood and Society*. New York: W.W. Norton and Company, 1986.

Tillich, Paul. *Biblical Wisdom and the Search for Ultimate Reality*. Chicago: University of Chicago Press, 1955.

Chapter 4

Allport, Gordon W. *The Individual and His Religion*. New York: The MacMillan Company, 1950.

Droege, Thomas A. "Developmental View of Faith," *Journal of Religion and Health* 11, no. 4, October 1972.

Kennedy, Eugene C. and Heckler, Victor J. *The Catholic Priest in the United States: Psychological Investigations*. Washington D.C.: United States Catholic Conference, 1972.

O'Dugan, Daniel. *Faith for Tomorrow*. Dayton, Ohio: Pflaum Press, 1969.

Second Vatican Council. *Pastoral Constitution on the Church in the Modern World: Gaudium Et Spes*. Boston: Pauline Books, 1965.

Chapter 5

Barth, Karl. *Evangelical Theology*. New York: Holt, Rinehart and Winston, 1963.

Helfaer, Philip M. *The Psychology of Religious Doubt*. Boston: Beacon Press, 1972.

Tillich, Paul. *The Dynamics of Faith*. New York: Harper Brothers, 1957.

Chapter 7

Coriden James A., *The Canonical Doctrine of Reception*. Available at http://www.arcc-catholic-rights.net/doctrine_of_reception.htm.

John Paul II, Apostolic Letter, *Ordinatio Sacerdotalis*, May 22, 1994. Available at http://www.vatican.va.

Yaker, Henri. "Time in the Biblical and Greek Worlds" in *The Future of Time*, Yaker, Osmond,
    Cheek, eds. Garden City: Anchor Books, Doubleday, 1972.

Chapter 8

Barron, Frank. "Diffusion, Integration, and Enduring Attention" in *Study of Lives*, White, Robert A., ed. New York, Prentice-Hall, 1963.

Chapter 9

O'Neill, Eugene Gladstone. *Long Day's Journey into Night*. New Haven: Yale University Press, 1st ed. 1956.